IDA LUPINO
in Paramount Pictures

Ida Lupino: Beyond the Camera

100th Birthday
Special Edition

Written by Mary Ann Anderson
with Ida Lupino

BearManor
Media

Albany, Georgia

Published in the USA by
BearManor Media
P.O. Box 71426
Albany, GA 31708
www.BearManorMedia.com

Softcover Edition
ISBN-10: 1-62933-277-1
ISBN-13: 978-1-62933-277-2

Designed by duffincreative.com

Printed in the United States of America

Ida Lupino:
Beyond the Camera

Table of Contents

Acknowledgements

I wish to acknowledge the following people for their contributions:

Ann Sperber
Vincent Sherman
Olivia de Havilland
Joan Fontaine
Mala Powers
Bea Arthur
and
Julie Grossman
Louis Antonelli

Academy of Motion Picture Arts and Sciences
Margaret Herrick Library

• •

A very special thank you to the legendary Ida Lupino. Without her
extraordinary help this book could never have been written!

Foreword

HOLLYWOOD HAS THE WELL-DESERVED REPUTATION for being one of the most cosmopolitan cities in the world; justly so, for it has attracted to its environment creative men from the far corners of the globe. The use of the word "men" rather than "people" is deliberate, for while Hollywood can be proud of its male cultural imports, I don't think it has shown the same progressive attitude about women until the 1960s and 1970s.

There was an absolute and iron-clad cast system in the film capital in the 1940s and 1950s which, it seems to me, had its primary purpose to exclude females. Women back then would be seen in public, appear on television, frequent night clubs, attend the fights, and smoke; but, within the towering citadels and sound stages of a motion picture studio, there were women-tight compartments to which they may gain access only over the dead bodies of a guard, as tightly disciplined as a king's.

Women, according to these stalwart defenders of male superiority, may not be film musical directors, cameramen, set designers, composers, assistant directors, directors, or production managers. The only sort of job encouragement some women got in the early days of Hollywood was the portrayal of women on the screen. Sometimes, I suspect we were resented for even this intrusion. In Hollywood, 'women's pictures' were those four-hankie soaps and cautionary tales directed by men, often based on works by lady novelists and translated to the screen with an eye towards the female demographics.

At this time, Warner Bros. was picking the most difficult roles for me to play; and the more difficult they became, the more I liked them.

Years ago, when my father was active on the London stage and in motion pictures, he once took me to the film studio at Elstree, where he was working. My tour included a visit to the cutting room, that chamber of decisions where a man with great big shears often decides the fate of actors and actresses. I watched the film editors at work, intrigued by the mechanics of what they were doing and a little awed by the fact that they were men who determined what went up on the screen.

Father made a remark. "Ida," he said, "the player whose likeness appears on those pieces of film is important; the man who determines what pieces is the most important of all. He is the director. Just remember that!"

I did remember it, and years later when I was under contract to Warner Bros., I received front-office permission to spend time in the studio cutting rooms. From time to time, one of the indulgent film editors would let me operate a movieola or splice some film, little experiences that served to implement my desires to become a part of the behind-the-scenes operation of motion pictures.

I was to wait nine years before my first opportunity came. In association with Collier Young, I co-produced a picture, *Not Wanted*, and used two new, unknown people in the cast, Sally Forrest and Keefe Brasselle. We made this picture for $110,000. The money men said they would not finance a second unless I directed. While working on *Not Wanted*, our director, the late and beloved Elmer Clifton, offered me the benefit of his long experience. I learned much from him and to him I was deeply grateful.

For it was decided that our next picture, *Outrage*, would mark my debut as a director. I would be the first woman to undertake such an assignment in more than ten years.

I arrived at the set at 7:30 in the morning, before any of the technicians would be there. The stage was empty, the set was dark, and I felt terribly alone. I asked myself over and over again, "Ida, just what do you think you're doing here?"

At 9:01 a.m. I remember saying "Action" and, as I heard the whirl of the camera and the players speak their lines, I realized that the entire irrevocable, unavoidable process had started. It was like a grinding machine that wouldn't stop. Things happened and a picture was being made.

I was grateful for our noon breaks, and I hid in the far end of the stage during that one-hour lunch period alone, worried and full of doubt. Just before we returned to continue the day's work, cameraman Archie Stout took me aside. "Just before I went to work for you, Ida, I did a picture for director John Ford. Now, there's a real worried guy before he starts shooting a picture. He can take lessons in composure from you."

I'm sure Archie made that up for my benefit, but I loved him for it, and I tried hard not to show my real concern. I can't say that I was the most comfortable person in the world when I directed pictures. I felt I had much to learn, but each experience made the job easier.

During *Hard, Fast and Beautiful*, my third directorial effort, we were barely making ends meet and had hocked our life insurance policies. Just as shooting began, the assistant director rushed to me and said our money men went broke! We had a $65,000.00 payroll to meet in two weeks. I kept smiling and lining up shots until 5 p.m. Then I called my agent, Charlie Feldman, and told him all about it. He said to send the script over. If he liked it, there would be $65,000.00 in the bank. Two hours later the money was there.

Fortunately, I was willing to make the sacrifice when I embarked on a production and directing career. I did not abandon my acting. Whenever producers offered me screen roles, I accepted, for even if I enjoyed being a lone woman in the world of movie executives, it was fun to be a pampered, fussed-over actress. I loved playing sexy, warm dames who are tough in life, who do not let life affect them, very much myself!

Action!

Ida as a little girl, age four.

1
The Lupino Legacy

"I was born on February 4, 1918 (not 1916), in Camberwell, England. My father, Stanley Lupino, was a comedian, playwright and stage producer. The Gaiety Theatre, in London, was owned by my father. My family had originally hailed from Italy and migrated to England in the 17th Century. We lived on 152 Leigham Court Road Streatham Hill, outside of London, on an acre and one half of land next door to the United Dairies, which was opposite the church. I went to school at the Claurence School in Sussex.

"In the 1930s, my father appeared in such productions as *Crazie Days, Love Lies* (in which he sang 'Tweet Tweet'), *Sporting Love* and *Love Race* with my mum. They made regular appearances in London's famed West End. My dear little mum, Connie Emerald O'Shay, was a vaudevillian actress. On my father's side of the family, I had a tradition of show business tracing back to the jugglers and strolling players of the Italian Renaissance period, when the name Lupino was known in the courts of nobility. My Uncles Harry, Mark and Cousin Lupino Lane also appeared on stage. For almost four centuries, all the famous Lupinos were men."

Ida was the first distaff member of the clan to achieve stardom. "From my earliest recollection, I was preparing for a career in show business. Theatre was so much a part of my family background that, instead of a doll's house, my father, Stanley, constructed a complete miniature theatre with dressing rooms in the back garden, where I learned the fundamentals of stage craft. This theatre was called The Tom Thumb Theatre and seated 150 people."

Ida had 'not wanted' to become an actress; composing and writing were her main interests. She composed a musical score called "Aladdin's Lamp," and it was performed by the Los Angeles Philharmonic under the direction of Maury Rubene.

"I had no desire to crash into a man's world. I knew it would break my father's heart if I did not go into the business. My father really wanted a son, but he felt that I would follow after him. I was a great admirer of my father and it was a great compliment that he felt that way about me— to write, to produce and to act. I wanted to be an extra on his pictures, to watch my father work! I would have broken his heart if I did not become an actress!"

"I made my professional debut when I was not quite fourteen years old. Director Allan Dwan saw me at the Royal Academy of Dramatic Arts. Vivian Leigh went there, too. I was picked for the role of a young girl in *Her First Affair*, opposite my Godfather, Ivor Novella (1932). Not at all true: my mum tested for the role! My screen career was launched—as a dirty little cockney slut."

Ida received more screen roles, small parts throughout the year— *Money For Speed, I Lived With You, Prince of Arcadia* and *Ghost Camera*. "*Ghost Camera* was my favorite film that I made in England. It starred John Mills. Years later, I would direct his daughter Hayley and George Merritt. I thought the script was very intriguing. A photographer takes a photo at the scene of a murder, and his camera is tossed out of a castle window to destroy evidence. It lands in the back seat of a passing car belonging to a chemist. John Gray becomes an amateur sleuth after developing the film and goes in search of the woman captured on the photograph—me!"

"I made these pictures before my mum brought me to Hollywood to do a screen test for the title role of *Alice in Wonderland*."

Ida was picked for this audition for her appearance in a film called *Money for Speed* (1933). Young as Ida was, she realized what the studio executives did—that she was not right for the part.

"Paramount scouts had heard of me. I played a dual role. They only saw the section where I was the sweet little blond, not the part when I was a hooker. I came to America with my mum. We came to America on the ship called *The Berengaria*. My father, Stanley, and sister, Rita, stayed behind in England. I did a make-up test for Paramount. I was in long, blond braids with bows, wearing a taffeta dress, white socks, and little black shoes. I sounded like Mae West with my deep voice. They would have to make the *Alice in Wonderland* picture a musical and have me dance on table tops.

"I found it exciting to be in Los Angeles. All I knew were the movies in England and if I could ever meet Gary Cooper, Wow! I saw him and I told him, 'You are gorgeous!' He said, 'Thank you, young lady.' I ended up doing a picture with him! And, Marlene Dietrich. I was a great fan of hers, along with W.C. Fields and Bing Crosby. I ended up doing a picture with Bing."

Ida's first American film was in 1934 with swimming champion Buster Crabbe and Clara Lou Sheridan.

"I played Barbara Hilton in *Search For Beauty*, made at Paramount Studios.

"Ann Sheridan, who was in the picture and changed her name from Claira Lou from my suggestion, was a beloved buddy of mine, a great gal. She later was known as 'The Oomph Girl.'"

Meet the Royal Family of Greasepaint

By Paul Harrison

There have been Lupinos on the stage for hundreds of years — in England since Shakespeare's time, in Italy much longer — so what more natural than that this oldest theatrical line of them all should invade Hollywood?

Stanley and Ida

Stanley signs autographs with Connie, Rita and Ida

Ida next appeared, also in 1934, in *Come On Marines*. "I portrayed Esther Smith-Hamilton, one of the shipwrecked women rescued by the Marines.

"In 1935, I appeared as the 'Heart of Interest' of Harold Lloyd in *The Milky Way*.

Connie and Ida

Buster Crabbe and Ida Lupino

This was my first big-screen chance, and I starred opposite this fine comedian in the Paramount Production of this popular play."

"In *Smart Girl*, I appeared with Kent Taylor and Joseph Cawthorn. This was a Walt Wanger Production made by Paramount."

"I appeared again in a film, titled *Peter Ibbetson*, where I co-starred with Ann Harding and Gary Cooper."

This film did not do well in the United States but was a success in Europe.

Ida appeared in her first musical in 1936, *Anything Goes*, co-starring Ethel Merman, Bing Crosby and Arthur Treacher.

"I played Hope Harcourt, an English heiress who is wooed by Crosby's character."

One of Ida's finest roles of this period was in *The Gay Desperado* (1936), co-starring Leo Carrillo and Nino Martini. This film was

The Milky Way

directed by Rouben Mamoulian, and under the control of Mary Pickford-Jesse L. Laske Productions and released by United Artists. This film was later restored by the UCLA Film and Television Archive and the Mary Pickford Foundation. It was rereleased in 2006 by Milestone Pictures on DVD. This film helped define Ida's early career.

"I spent most of my time in this film being tied up. What a title! Can you imagine making a picture with that title today?"

"It was 1937 when I did a picture with Jack Benny called "Artists and Models." I was under contract to Paramount at $1,700.00 a week. They'd bleached me bright platinum blond, plucked out my eyebrows and penciled new ones on, made my face dead white, almost like a mask, and painted on red lips. In those days they'd take four months to shoot a picture and we were forever sitting around waiting to be called, so we gabbed a lot."

Bing Crosby and Ida in *Anything Goes*

Matinee Scandal poster. Credit: The Louis Antonelli Collection

"One day Hedda Hopper said to me, 'What do you really want to do? Do you want to be an actress?' I said, I wasn't sure, I suppose so.

"'Well,' she said, 'if you want to become a real actress, the first thing is to let your eyebrows grow, get your hair back to its natural shade, and scrub all that goo off of your face. Otherwise, you'll be just another starlet who fell by the wayside.'

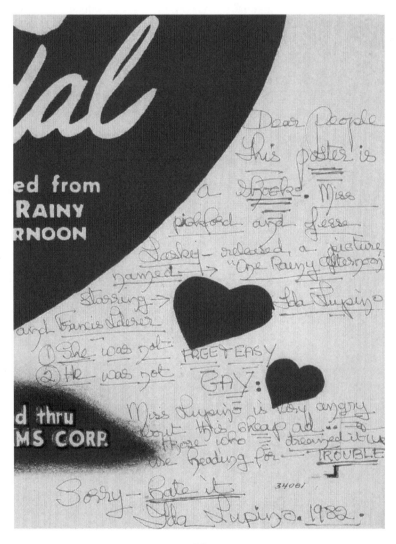

Gay Desperado

"Right after this I was offered a bit in *Cleopatra*. I was given something like five lines and was supposed to stand behind Claudette Colbert and wave a big palm frond. I said, 'No, thanks!' Paramount was shocked. 'You're under contract. You can't do this.' I told them I was finished with things like that! 'Ok,' said Paramount, 'you're suspended.'"

Ida walked out on her $1,700.00 per-week contract.

"I kept alive on radio and fared very well. I worked every solitary week doing radio on *Silver Theater* with Charles Boyer, on his show, and with Tyrone Power and C.B. De Mille on his *Lux Theatre*. I was off the screen for eighteen months and kept repeating, 'No, no, no' to every offer."

Ida on CBS Radio

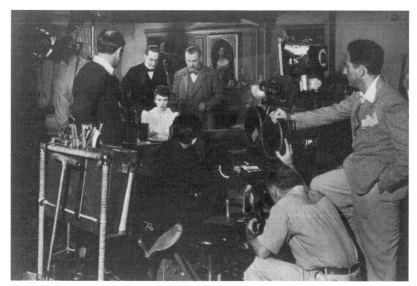

Sherlock Holmes set production

Lady and the Mob

Ida stars in *Sherlock Holmes*

Ida and Tommy Brown

Ida and her sister Rita

Ida wanted to prove she was a dramatic actress. In 1939 she appeared in *The Lone Wolf Spy Hunt* with Rita Hayworth and *Lady and the Mob*, directed by Benjamin Stoloff and filmed by Columbia. Ida co-starred with Fay Bainter and Lee Bowman in this film. Its concern was a society woman, Hattie Leonard, who organized her own band of 'gang-busters' when she discovered that a garment she had sent to the dry cleaners had been taxed 25 cents to pay for gang protection.

"I later appeared in *The Adventures of Sherlock Holmes* for Twentieth Century-Fox."

"I loved working at Fox! Basil Rathbone, I thought, was great. I used to call him "Basil Bathrug" when he was deep in thought. Nigel Bruce was a darling and a dear friend. We had fun, great fun."

Ida was invited to get away and recuperate from a bad cold at the Bruce's country home, which turned out to be one block from her home in Beverly Hills.

Her young career was interrupted by a severe case of polio.

"It was at the time of an epidemic. I got hit with it. There was a six-day and six-night crisis, and there was a shortage of trained nurses. My mum took over and, within three weeks, I was out of danger. The doctors wanted wet sand bags next to me while I had polio so I would not move around. When they took the sand bags away, I could walk. It did leave me with the loss of some hearing in my right ear and my right hand does not open as well as my left."

"Ida had returned home from a date with Tommy Brown. She wasn't feeling well so Tommy left. I had recently read about the polio epidemic and was aware of the symptoms." - Connie Lupino

2
The Light That Failed

IDA WENT AFTER AND WAS CAST in the role of "Bessie" in *The Light That Failed* (1932), co-starring Ronald Colman, directed by maverick filmmaker William Wellman, and based on the timeless story by Rudyard Kipling. Paramount wanted Vivian Leigh for the part.

"Bill Wellman was looking through the book at Paramount, noticed my picture and called me in to read for *The Light That Failed* with Ronnie Colman. I was desperate by then. The studio had planned to drop my option when it came due."

"When Wellman called, I had my own hair and eyebrows and had lost weight. After the reading, he said, 'I'm not going to test you. You have the role. And, I have a .22. If you do not come through for me, I'll shoot out every light on the set and maybe you, too.' He brought me back to Paramount at three times my former salary and got me a dressing room on the first floor. Nothing could have been sweeter. It wasn't such a large role, but it was colorful."

William Wellman stated that Ronald Colman opposed Ida Lupino's casting as the vicious little cockney model and tried subtly

Ida and Ronald Colman

The Light That Failed scene still

and unsuccessfully to sabotage her scenes. The intensity of Ida's performance, particularly in the scene in which her character goes insane, completely overshadows the scenes of Ronald Colman.

"After the preview, I was driving along Sunset Boulevard. A red light stopped me and there was Hedda. 'All right,' she yelled, 'what did I tell you!' Hedda did not predict that after *The Light That Failed* I would go into oblivion again, so back to radio I went."

"Hedda and I remained close friends for many years. She went on to become a successful columnist. Hedda never wrote anything in her column that was not true about me."

The New York Times hailed her work: "Ida Lupino's Bessie is another of the surprises we get when a little ingénue bursts forth as a great actress."

The critical acclaim for *The Light That Failed* established Ida as an actress of the first rank, and she later emphasized that talent is subsequent films.

Dearest Ida,

How are you and Louis. Both well I hope. All your notices were fine for The Light. And just as good for Sherlock Holmes too. I see you have gone a real Brunette. I like it. I also read you are going to play in "Victory." That is interesting. I hope you will & very happy in the part— our show is going well still. But most of the cast with the flue. Still we are going along. I have money for Connie, but can't get over at the moment—government restrictions. But it is all here. So if she wants anything let her—her wine, anything she wants. I would like to see your new home.

Someday I expect, —O' shall let me have all the news when you can. I like to hear whats going on out there. The Sun is shinning again here so we feel more up and going. It's wonderful what a bell of Sun means over here. We get so tired of the continuous Black But I've got an idea. This year will see I over.

Give my love to all of your pals. Tons of love to you and Louis

Dad XXX

XXXX

XXX

3
They Drive By Night

"I got a call from Warner's to test for *They Drive By Night*, which co-starred Humphrey Bogart, George Raft, and Ann Sheridan. Raoul Walsh and Mark Hellinger gave me the part. Mark was wonderful to me. I wished he would have stayed on at Warner's. I was called in, and Warner's asked me to sign a seven-year contract."

"I said I would have to think it over. All I could think of was that seven years from that day I'd be a movie star, but they'd be saying the same thing to another girl—that in seven years she'd be another Ida Lupino.

"I decided there was something more for me in life than being a big star, so I said 'No' and walked out."

"I went ahead and appeared in *They Drive By Night* (1940). This picture shoved me to the top. I murder my husband, played by Alan Hale." Then Ida laughed, "The doors made me do it!"

Bosley Crowther in *The New York Times*, wrote: "Miss Lupino goes crazy about as well as it can be done."

They Drive By Night George, Ida, Ann & Bogie.
Credit: Warner Bros. Studio

They Drive by Night candid set still

Ida steals the picture from co-stars George Raft and Humphrey Bogart.

"I got along very well with George Raft. He was very good at what he was doing in this picture. Many years later, we co-starred in *Deadend Miles*. I really didn't get to know Bogie well on this picture—we didn't have any scenes together—but Ann Sheridan and I were buddies."

This time Warner Bros. decided to lock up her services, and Ida signed a seven-year contract with the studio. Her years at Warner Bros. brought her much success and frustration.

According to Jack Warner's memoir, Ida stayed away during most of the filming of *They Drive By Night* because an astrologer had told her that the film would be bad luck. One-half million dollars had been spent, and the crew was put on another picture before she returned.

Warner implies that Lupino was not a very easy star to handle.

Ida only stayed at Warner's for six years, but she turned out several memorable dramatic portrayals during that time. She worked with several fine directors—Raoul Walsh, Michael Curtiz and Vincent Sherman among them. Her most iconic work as an actress may have been during this period.

"I worked against my (commercial) success by refusing to do roles that I did not believe in," she stated.

Ida also refused to work with actors who failed to respect her personally or professionally.

4
High Sierra

Ida Lupino starred in *High Sierra,* receiving star billing above Humphrey Bogart.

"*High Sierra* was a damn good role for me. When Bogie sends Marie and Pard out of town on the bus, I could not cry. Bogie tried to help me and asked me when did I last lose something? I still couldn't make it happen, so Bogie said, 'Just think about the way it might be; you may never see Pard and me, again.' The tears came. When I had to cry over his body at the end of the picture, I could do it. They were real tears!"

"As for Bogie's acting style? Real. Real every moment. I used to tease him, 'You are not going to break my arm?' Bogie said we were all rotten at Warner Bros. and the audience is going to love us! Bogie was right."

Ann Sperber, author of the biography entitled *Bogart,* wrote, "According to Irving Rapper, the dialogue coach on the set of *High*

Sierra, Bogie was crazy about Ida! The scene up at the tourist camp where Marie brings Earl breakfast on a tray and he gets her whole story out of her is incredibly written (by John Huston) and very well performed by both Ida and Bogie."

It was not just Humphrey Bogart's performance as Mad Dog Earle, but Raoul Walsh's taut, yet sensitive, direction that makes the picture come alive. The close-up scene at the end of the film, in which Marie is torn between relief and grief while holding her little dog, Pard, is excellent. This character was devoted to Bogart's doomed gangster. Ida's tremendous one word, "Free," in the closing moments of this film stands alone in the lexicon of cinema in the 1940s.

"I thought Raoul Walsh was just great," she said. "I called him 'Uncle.' It was wonderful working with men. 'Pard' (given name 'Zero') was Bogie's dog in real life, so it was easy for 'Pard' to run over to his body at the end of the picture."

William Whitebait, critic, wrote, "Ida Lupino gives us the best moll I have ever seen."

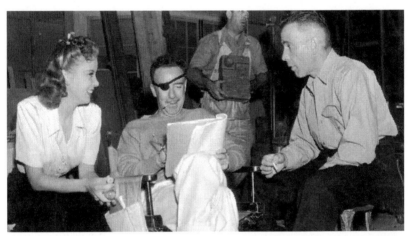

Ida and Bogie on the set of *High Sierra* with Raoul Walsh, Director:
"I received billing above Bogie!" — *Ida Lupino*

Credit: The Louis Antonelli Collection

On the set of *The Sea Wolf*

5

The Sea Wolf – Out of the Fog – Ladies in Retirement – Moontide

"I appeared in *The Sea Wolf* and *Out of the Fog* for Warner Bros., both First National Pictures. My expression in this photo is strictly acting! I am rehearsing a scene with John Garfield, while visitor Jack Haley listens with his eyes closed," Ida laughs.

Ida recalls *Out of the Fog*, "Warner Bros. was absolutely lying, completely untrue, completely untrue. I did want Bogie cast in *Out Of the Fog*; however, John Garfield ended up with the gangster role in this picture. John was a beautiful performer."

Ida starred in *Ladies in Retirement* (1941) for Columbia, produced by Lester Cowan and Gilbert Miller, co-starring Louis Hayward, Isobel Elson, Edith Barrett and Elsa Lanchester.

"I play a steely housekeeper who murders my employer, a vulgar ex-actress, rather than have my two sisters put away."

"I appeared in *The Sea Wolf* with Edward G. Robinson (1942) for Twentieth Century–Fox. I found Robinson to be the toughest one on the lot. We did not have any warm feelings for each other. When we worked together, it was easy for us to hate each other, and we continued that way!"

Ida and John Garfield

Cast photo *Ladies In Retirement*

Garfield, Lupino & Robinson

Ida and Louis, happy for a while

6
Louis Hayward

Born in Johannesburg, Hayward began his screen work in British films, notably as Simon Templar in Leslie Charteris's *The Saint in New York*. In 1939, Louis played the career-defining dual role in *The Man in the Iron Mask.*

Ida's marriage to Louis Hayward lasted until May 11, 1945, when Ida made an emotional two-minute court appearance and a charge of extreme mental cruelty to win her divorce from Louis, who had been discharged from the Marine Corps. as a Captain.

"We had been married seven years. We married in 1938." Personal letter to Ida from Louis:

> "Little One…You see how impossible the whole thing is…I realized this morning when you didn't seem to want me to even stay in the house that it was no good…I don't blame you at all, because my behavior was rather absurd… but that is the way I always seem to get when I am with you…you have stood for a great deal of this kind of thing

Ida in Court

and this really makes me terribly sad, but there's nothing I can do about myself...You see the very last thing I want to do is to hurt you in any way at all, but I continue to do so it appears...This MUST cease...and there seems only the one course open...When you or I take this step, I shall see that you are protected, because it is wrong for anyone to drag you down, and make you appear as a dreadful character...I shall tell the press that it was something we decided to do long before I went overseas...

...Darling I REALLY am sorry that I behave in such an abject way, but you know why I do, and that there is nothing I can do about it, except to get out of your life once and for all...Believe me I will never hurt anybody the way I said I would last night, or rather this morning...I'm a complete nitwit to talk like that...sorry.

...Darling, darling...I ask you to forgive me, and you better pray that you NEVER meet anyone who loves you in the heart breaking, and dreadful way I do...

Louis

Captain Louis Hayward directed the Marine photographic unit during the Battle of Tarawa in 1943. They filmed it for a documentary titled *With the Marines at Tarawa*. This documentary won the 1944 Academy Award for Best Documentary-Short Subject. Louis was given the Bronze Medal.

"When he returned home he was 'shell shocked.' Louis was experiencing severe psychological effects from exposure to warfare, especially shell fire. His unit had to photograph all of this and it severely affected Louis. I loved him. I was deeply crushed when he asked me to divorce him."

WESTERN UNION

SC23 NL PD=TDS BEVERLY HILLS CALIF 20

MISS IDA LUPINO=

SHERRY-NETHERLANDS HOTEL NYK=

A TINY PART OF YOU IN A YELLOW JACKET SLIPPED GRACEFULLY
UNDER MY DOOR LAST NIGHT THANKYOU. I SAT ALONE IN YOUR
HOUSE FOR TWO HOURS THIS EVENING PLAYING BACHS HEBREW
RHAPSODY, UNDER THESE CIRCUMSTANCES SLIGHT NOSTALGIA
INEVITABLE YOUR BRILPRESENCE HAS ALREADY PERMEATED THE PLACE
STIMULATING AND WONDERFUL GIRL. KEEP YOUR HEAD AND

ASPIRATIONS HIGH AND NEVER FALTER IN YOUR GOOD TASTE.
LET NO NEBULOUS UNIMPORTANT EMOTION ROB YOU OF ALL THOSE
THINGS STANLEY BEQUEATHED YOU. PERHAPS MY JOB IS DONE AND
YOU HAVE OUTRUN ME. YET ALWAYS REMEMBER LOVE CAN FUNCTION
STANDING ON THE SIDE LINES SO BABY I'LL BE WATCHING YOU AND
CHEERING YOU ON, AND IF ANY CHARACTER FORGETS MARQUIS OF
QUEENSBURY RULES LET HIM BEWARE. GOD BE WITH YOU. ABOUT
THIS TIME CALIFORNIA IS ENVYING NEW YORK. GO TO IT GIRL=

LOUIS.

During the war Ida, a Lieutenant, was in charge of dispatching emergency air raid ambulances from her home, for the Los Angeles area.

"I was commissioned by the American Ambulance Corps. I was required to wear a uniform at all times, to and from the studio, except when I was before the camera. I even learned to drive an ambulance!"

"My family home in England had been damaged by the blasts of war. The bombings in the neighborhood had seriously damaged the underpinning, most of the windows were blown in and most everything in ruins!"

Captain Louis Hayward at Tarawa 12/4/43 Credit: Associate Press

Ida dispatching ambulances.

Ida in uniform receives an emergency call.

1
The Hard Way

A Warner Brothers Production -
Jack L. Warner in Charge of Production Produced by Jerry Wald
Directed by Vincent Sherman
Screen Play by Irwin Shaw and Daniel Fuchs Original Story
   by Jerry Wald
Fictionalized by Gwen Jones

Helen Chernen.............. Ida Lupino
Katherine Chernen........Joan Leslie
Paul Collins..........Dennis Morgan
Albert Runkel..........Jack Carson

Plot: "A question was once asked in a very old book. Occasionally someone tries to answer that question; but if anyone has found the answer, he hasn't said so. The question reads: For what shall it profit a man if he gain the whole world and lose his own soul? Only one answer can be found in the ruthless of heart. Defeat!"

"I know what she is...

and I despise her for it!"

Dennis Morgan

Joan Leslie

A GREAT **WARNER BROS.** PICTURE

Ida Lupino

One couldn't get them out of his mind— the other out of his heart!

They Learned About Love

"THE HARD WAY"

...the way most women learn about Love

with JACK CARSON · GLADYS GEORGE · FAYE EMERSON · Directed by VINCENT SHERMAN · Screen Play by Daniel Fuchs and Peter Viertel

December 1942 Good Housekeeping

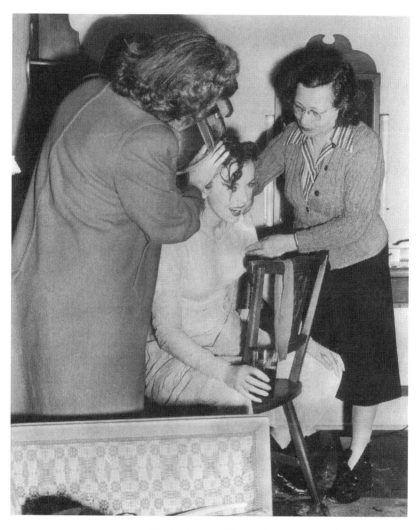

"Prelude to a Plunge"
Warner Bros. Studios Burbank, California. Credit: Mac Julian

Helen Chernen wasn't thinking of the Bible when she and her sister, Katherine, stood in front of the shop window, staring at the white graduation dress displayed there. The only question in Helen's mind was how she was going to get that dress for her little sister. Katherine wanted it so much. Graduation from high school is an important event for a young girl, especially in Greenhill, Pennsylvania, where the grime and squalor and everyday poverty make every day life a pretty dismal affair.

"Though *The Hard Way*, directed by one of my favorite directors, Mr. Vincent Sherman, did a great deal for my career as an actress, when I saw the picture at the preview, I could not stand looking at my own scenes. I thought the other actors in it were magnificent but that my own performance was incredibly bad. I walked out in the middle of it. My portrayal of Helen Chernen, a grim and bitter witch, earned me The New York Critic's Award, that year. I guess I should have stayed and watched the entire picture!"

"I leaped into the river, fully clothed, for a scene in *The Hard Way*, but my scenes that show me after my plunge were filmed in a warm, studio sound stage. I was drenched before every take!"

Vincent Sherman, director of *The Hard Way*, recalls, "I insisted that the actors, including women, wear no makeup during the opening scenes. I wanted the freckles, sweat and blemishes to come through. At first Ida hesitated, but she finally went along.

"After a few days of seeing the rushes, Ida became concerned because she thought she looked too greasy and messy; and since she was playing a bitter, frustrated woman, Ida began to worry how the audiences would accept her. One day while filming an exterior shot, Ida stormed onto the set and declared, 'This picture is going to stink and I am going to stink in it!' I wanted her to be mean and nasty in this picture. 'I do not want to be such a bitch in this,' Ida proclaimed.

"Midway through the picture Ida received word from London that her father, Stanley, had died. She was distraught and we went through some difficult days with her. While we were shooting at an old studio of Warner's in the Los Feliz area, where there was a theatre and a stage, in leaping back and forth from the stage to the audience area, where I had set up a camera, I threw my back out. I was in a great deal of pain; the emotional intensity of the story and my struggle to keep the conflict always at white heat plus Ida's insecurity and grief for her father caused a strain between us.

"The problems grew between us and during the last few weeks of the picture we were not even speaking to each other. After *The Hard Way* premiered to rave reviews, Mark Hellinger telephoned me. 'Have you seen the reviews Vincent, raving about the picture? Ida got sensational reviews! Give her a call.' Ok, sure I will call her. Well, late that night or the next morning I called Ida. 'Hello Ida. This is Vincent Sherman.' Ida's telephone greeting, 'Hello Darling, how are you?'"

Excerpt from a personal letter from Vincent to Ida:

12/29/93
Dearest Ida,

"...Your characterization, the energy and drive from frustrated housewife to successful mentor of your young sister was relenting but your vulnerability and yearning for love and affection were most revealing when Dennis Morgan kisses you in that scene in the doorway just after you have separated Leslie and Jack Carson. In fact, every scene displayed a different facet of your character and was intriguing."

"It was a tribute to your towering talent and at any other studio besides Warner's, who didn't appreciate the film, you would have been nominated by the Academy...I wanted to tell you how much I really admired you."

Your sincere admirer Much Love
Vincent

Ida wardrobe test *The Hard Way*

Vincent and Ida on the set of *The Hard Way*

Life Begins at 8:30 Ida and Monty Wooley

8
Life Begins at 8:30

"MONTY WOOLEY, A DELIGHT TO WORK WITH as my father. I was a club-foot girl, my father a wonderful Shakespearian actor, but an alcoholic character, too drunk to get roles. My big scene hiding all of the bottles except one and he discovers this. I want him to think he drank all of the other bottles. My father starts looking for a drink.

"During filming and Monty's big scene, Monty starts, 'Failure, my child has emancipated me as surely as Lincoln 'screwed' the slaves.'The director and crew were stunned! Monty said, 'This is a dull picture and this will jazz it up!'

"Monty was my buddy in real life. We attended the *Pied Piper* Premiere together at The Chinese Theater in 1942."

Life Begins at 8:30 Ida and Monty Wooley

Pied Piper premiere, Ida and Monty Wooley

9
Starry Efforts

IDA APPEARED IN THREE STARRY EFFORTS for RKO. The first was *Forever and a Day.*

"*Forever and a Day* was an all-star feature produced by Sir Cedric Hardwicke with an unprecedented assembly of top-ranking stars, directors, writers and technicians, all donating services to old British and American charities. RKO Radio Pictures released this film without profits. Bravo RKO!"

"*Thank Your Lucky Stars*, where I jitterbug with Olivia De Havilland. Musical comedy like my Father!"

Ann Sperber: "Bogie was to be in this skit but he was working on a picture for Columbia so they used George Tobias instead. Ida did this skit with such flair. Olivia really struggles through this. Ida could out dance and sing me!"

Olivia de Havilland: "That is why I chewed gum!"

Hollywood Canteen, Warner Bros. (1944), starring Joan Leslie, Robert Hutton and Dane Clark. This film received three Academy Award nominations. "This film's setting is The Hollywood Canteen,

Forever and a Day

a free entertainment club open to service men. I appeared in a brief skit in a theatrical commercial, 'To stay on the job and finish the job for Victory.'" The canteen was created as a G.I. morale booster by Bette Davis and John Garfield during World War II.

"*In Our Time*, I was as an English woman in love with a Polish aristocrat, Paul Henreid, at the time of the Nazi invasion… directed by Vincent Sherman."

Vincent Sherman said, "Ida called me and asked me if I would like to direct this picture? I read the script and I agreed to direct it. This was a hard subject to do, the Nazi's invading Poland. The story never really turned out the way I wanted it to. There were certain aspects of this picture that were very good. Ida did everything that I asked her to do this time. She was no longer the hard-driven, ruthless character of

The Hard Way, but a warm, shy, romantic, enchanting young idealistic. Ida did it beautifully, what a pleasure working on this picture with her."

Olivia, George and Ida in *Thank Your Lucky Stars*

"In 1945, I made *Pillow to Post,* Vincent Sherman's army comedy. I loved working with Vincent, again. I co-starred with Sidney Greenstreet and William Prince. I got the most fan mail ever from our boys overseas." Vincent Sherman: "I phoned Ida and told her the story and suggested she might enjoy doing this. Ida read it and liked it. The script had great lines:

Jean Howard: "Love is a beautiful thing."
Lieutenant Don Mallory: "I get two hours of it every
    Saturday night at a movie. That's enough for me."

"I had never done a farce or comedy, nor had Ida, but I was confident she could do it. I had seen her antics when she was in a playful mood and I knew how to get laughs. This was a very fun picture to make, all of the gags, the bed and the ironing board. Soldiers just loved this film. Ida was delightful. There wasn't any kind of part that she couldn't have done, comedy or drama."

Paul Heinreid and Ida on the set of *In Our Time*

Pillow to Post

Devotion: The Bronte Family

Devotion: The Bronte Family

Devotion

10
Devotion – The Man I Love – Deep Valley – Escape Me Never – Road House – Lust For Gold

"*Devotion*, Curtis Bernhardt's expressive lumbering film about the Bronte Family. I portray Emily Bronte, and I enjoyed working again with Olivia de Havilland, who portrays Charlotte. I play a good woman in this for a change, Emily Bronte."

Films that followed were *The Man I Love* (1946) with Robert Alda, directed by Roual Walsh.

"Excellent film. I play a torch singer.

Ida and Arthur Kennedy

The Man I Love

Road House Cormel Wilde, Richard Wydmark, Ida Lupino

Road House

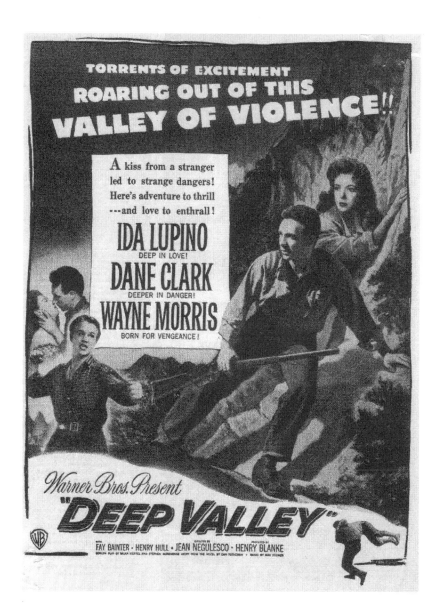

Deep Valley (1947)

"I did not want to do this picture because I felt the script was too similar to *High Sierra*. Warner Bros. wanted to capitalize on this. I insisted on script changes, even though the critics and the audiences noticed the similarities. I played a back-woods girl with a speech impediment. My changes gave this film a rustic feel. Dane Clark co-starred."

Escape Me Never (1947)

"I play a European peasant girl weeping over Errol Flynn. Errol gave a beautiful performance in this film. Eleanor Parker co-stars. This was my last film for Warner Bros. I was thrilled to get away from them!"

"In 1948 I became an American citizen and, in the very same year, I played another torch singer in *Road House* (1948) with Richard Widmark, Cornel Wilde and Celeste Holm. Using my own voice, I sing a song titled 'Again.' I was asked to sing at night clubs after this picture opened."

Ida and Errol at lunch

Ida and Cornel Wilde share an embrace in *Road House*

Ida Directing *Screen Director Playhouse*

Four Star Playhouse

This show featured four rotating stars, Charles Boyer, David Niven and Dick Powell in individual episodes from comedy to drama.

Release date: September 28, 1952

"I was the guest that came to dinner and stayed!" - Ida Lupino

Owned by Four Star International. These shows were sponsored during its bi-weekly season by The Singer Company. Bristol - Meyers became an alternative sponsor, when it became a weekly series in the fall of 1953.

"I was in nineteen episodes and became a partner of four Star." - Ida Lupino

In 1954, *Billboard* voted it the second best filmed network television drama series.

"I wrote two episodes in 1956." - Ida Lupino

Lust for Gold

Ida appeared in a Western for Columbia Pictures titled *Lust for Gold*, a screen adaptation of Barry Storm's autobiography, which told of a prolonged search for gold in Arizona. Glenn Ford who co-starred, sang for the very first time in *Lust for Gold*.

"I co-star along with Gig Young. Gig and I are having a quick snack while Glenn tunes up on his song."

Ida and Gig on the set of *Lust for Gold*

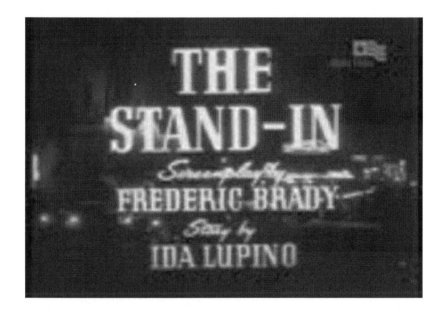

11
The Filmakers

REFUSING TO PLAY ONE DIMENSIONAL CHARACTERS—prostitutes, maids and torch singer roles, Ida Lupino began writing, producing, directing, and sometimes starring in films for her own production company.

"I had largely given up on acting and turned to producing and directing. This gave me the freedom to call my own shots."

And, Ida's status grew to genuine Auteur Filmmaker.

"I learned a lot form George Barnes, a marvelous cameraman."

Jack Edmond Nolan in a *Film Fan Monthly* article would judge her: " uniquely among women directors, she had a successful acting career behind her and ahead of her, when in 1947 at age thirty-one, she obtained her director's 'ticket.'"

"I held my own in the toughest kind of man's world. I joined with Anson Bond, of the Bond clothing firm, in writing and producing."

In 1949, Ida Lupino and her then-husband, Collier Young, formed an independent film company named Emerald Productions after Ida's mother, Connie Emerald O'Shay. It was later renamed, as a defining statement of intent, Filmakers.

The Filmakers Company 1949 to 1954

"Collier Young served as the company's president and I was the vice president."

Collier had been an executive assistant to Columbian head Harry Cohn. Filmakers made eight pictures, six of which Ida directed.

"Believe me, I fought to produce and direct my own pictures."

"I co-authored with Paul Jarrico *Not Wanted.* This film tells the story, powerfully, frankly, in all its pathetic detail, through the eyes and tears of one girl, willful and beautiful. Sally, who wanted so much out of life and who knew so little of it either. The story of Sally is a page taken from life.

"When I was preparing for a motion picture role which I was studying, I did research at a police court in Los Angeles. I was engaged in first-hand observation of a pretty girl in her mid-teens, who was brought in by a policewoman. The girl had been picked up for loitering on the street. The sharp eye of the police officer detected she was pregnant.

"Later, in the judge's chamber, the whole national picture was painted for me, of the 100,000 girls, half of them between ten and nineteen years old, who bring children into the world outside wedlock each year. I determined the story, shocking though it was, had to be brought to the screen.

"I had to use my star power and negotiate with the Production Code representatives to get *Not Wanted* made."

Direction of this picture is credited to Elmer Clifton, who, three days into production, suffered a heart attack. Ida took over the film's direction. The film's subject was controversial. It received a vast amount of publicity. "I was invited to discuss the film with Eleanor Roosevelt on radio!" - Ida Lupino

"I wanted to make films with good stories and new faces."

Several other films followed: *Outrage; Never Fear, aka The Young Lovers; Private Hell 36; Hard, Fast and Beautiful; The Bigamist; The Hitch-Hiker;* and *Beware My Lovely.* These were sensational subjects for the time, but they were treated with restraint and with unsentimental realism—a real break from Hollywood aesthetics. The Production Code Administration PCA was in full force.

Mala Powers, star of *Outrage*, said, "I met Ida and read for *Outrage.* She was an excellent director; she would protect you. If you dared to be original and try things, she was there for you. She was a wonderful friend. There was always a lot of laughter. Ida Lupino was not a feminist."

On the set of *Never Fear* (re-titled *The Young Lovers* shortly after its initial release), while directing on location at the Kabet Kaiser Institute in Santa Monica, Ida and her film crew fell from the high parallel 125 feet to the ground. Ida's main camera was up there.

"The parallel swayed. No arc lights were attached, thank God. All three of us were up there—Archie, Jim and me. We needed to leave quietly. I thought the whole damn thing was going to collapse. Archie started first, I followed and Jim went the other side. The damn thing collapsed!

Ida and Mala on the set of *Outrage*

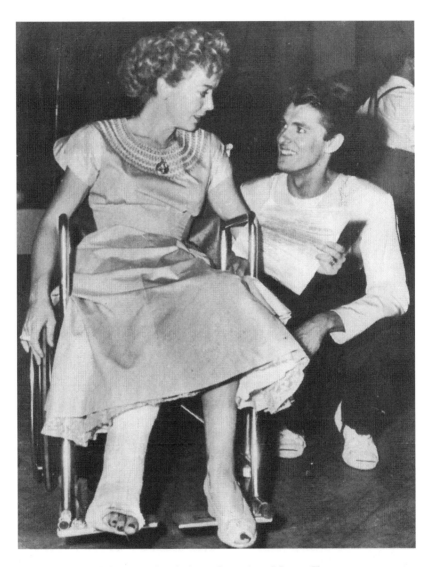

Ida in a wheel chair directing *Never Fear*

We went down and hit the pads on the floor. I knew I was in trouble with my ribs and ankle. I tried to move but I could not. I was in agony, and so were Archie and Jim. Medical help came with stretchers. I broke my ribs, right ankle and injured my right knee. Archie and Jim had bad injuries. I ended up directing this film in a wheelchair."

Hard, Fast and Beautiful and *The Hitch-Hiker* are considered to be Ida's best directorial efforts of this period. Ida composed an original piano selection for *Outrage*, entitled "Didn't You Know."

Ida: "She was electric," says Sally Forrest, whom I'd discovered and directed in three pictures, including *Not Wanted*. "She never had the popularity she should have had. She was beautiful. She had a fabulous figure and a great director. Maybe she was too strong for those days."

Filmakers proceeded with their new crime drama, *Private Hell 36*. Ida and Collier Young co-wrote this script, which was geared toward greed and cops. The script cast Howard Duff and Steve Cochran as detectives, investigating counterfeit cash.

Record cover *Private Hell 36*

"I starred as a night-club singer who receives a fake bill as a tip."

Ida starred in *Beware My Lovely* for Filmakers with Robert Ryan.

"I am discussing the intensity of this scene with director Harry Horner."

"I am reacting to the approaching footsteps after a day of terror in the house."

During Lupino's marriage to Collier Young, Collier became involved with Ida's close friend Joan Fontaine, who was married to television producer William Dozier, from whom she was separated at the time.

"I used to come home and find blond hair on my pillow," Ida complained.

Collier Young, Ida & Robert Ryan

Joan Fontaine, "Ida may of resented me marrying Collier Young, though we never discussed it!"

Ida and Collier divorced in 1950, a decision Ida always regretted.

"Filmakers was doing fine but we made one fatal mistake. We were talked into the distribution business. I opposed them every step of the way. We were creative people, we were picture-making people, I argued. 'We know nothing about distribution. Let's stay away from it.' I was outvoted, and pretty soon we were out of business."

On the set of *Beware My Lovely* "Talking things over"

Filmakers, with Ida the only woman in the room

"Sound of terror" *Beware My Lovely*

With the collapse of Filmakers, Ida was forced to find acting jobs. Producer Bryon Foy starred her as a sadistic warden in *Women's Prison* (1955). Howard Duff was cast as the prison doctor.

"I enjoyed playing the vicious warden, but I insisted on stylish dresses, earrings and jewelry. It makes my character look crueler."

Woman's Prison

12
Enter Howard Duff

IDA STARTED SEEING HOWARD DUFF. He was the son of a Bremerton, Washington wholesale grocer. Howard's first taste of theatre was in a production of "Trelawney of the Well" in his senior year at Roosevelt High School in Seattle, Washington. Shortly after his high-school graduation, he joined the Seattle Repertory Playhouse and received experience performing various Shakespearean roles in the group's productions. Howard was a non-salaried actor and found it necessary to seek regular employment. His low, poised speaking voice proved to be a valuable asset, winning him a job as staff announcer at Station KOMO. This permitted him to continue his Playhouse activities.

When, after a full year's employment, the theatre put Howard on salary at twenty dollars per week, he quit KOMO. He went on tour in the Northwest with the Playhouse productions. One such tour ended in San Francisco and, there, Duff found a role as the Phantom Pilot in a children's serial broadcast.

Shortly before the United States' entry into World War II, Howard went into the army. He served until November 1945 with the Armed

Forces Radio Service in Saipan, Guam and Iwo Jima. Howard Duff was honorably discharged and returned to radio work.

Howard continued to polish his acting talents at the Actor's Lab in Hollywood, where he had a prominent role in their production of *Birthday*.

During this period, Duff received several film offers, but turned them down because they were all stock contracts. Howard wanted to choose the roles he would play. In May 1946, he auditioned and was hired for the role of detective Sam Spade. This radio program went on the air in July 1946.

Hollywood opened doors for him after Howard earned a reputation on radio as Sam Spade. This proved to be a turning point in his career. He finally entered motion pictures in 1947, making his debut in *Brute Force*.

Ida recalled, "I was in love with his voice. I used to listen to him as Sam Spade on the radio." Even when they first met, on the set of *Woman in Hiding* in 1949, Ida and Howard had taken an instant dislike to each other. Ida thought Howard was "conceited." Howard thought Ida was "phony."

"Backstage shot, I am going over my script with director Michael Gordon in the background. Cameraman William Daniels contemplates his next setup for Universal-International's *Woman In Hiding*. Not one of my favorite pictures at all. If I would have never done this picture, I wouldn't have gotten involved with Duff. I regret ever marrying him!"

Ida soon became pregnant, and quickly divorced her husband Collier Young. Ida and Howard's daughter, Bridget, was born six months after they were married in 1951.

Collier and Joan were the Godparents for Ida and Howard's daughter, Bridget. They were married 1952.

Woman in Hiding film set production

Ida embarked on a new career in the dramatic anthology program *Four Star Playhouse*. Ida teamed up with David Niven, Dick Powell, and Charles Boyer, becoming the fourth star featured in its productions.

Ida and Howard separated in 1953. Ida told Louella Parsons, "The first six years of marriage are the hardest."

In a very personal letter to Howard, Ida wrote:

"Dear Howard, Believe me I really hate having to keep writing these notes to you, but I have no other way of communicating. Nanny delivered one up to the Franklin house but I have not the vaguest idea if you received it or ever will. I can't believe that after nearly four years of knowing me, and two and a half years of marriage, that you can leave me without some means of getting in touch with you. I realize this is probably the way you wish it right now-but-surely you could get yourself a call service that would deliver you messages. I have no idea where I stand at this time. I am Mrs. Howard Duff-in name only. I have no rights legally-to lead any other kind of life."

Ida and Howard reconciled. Ida recalled, "I guess we both decided to grow up! What made Howard so difficult to live with," she explained, "was that he was a really confirmed bachelor type, unaccustomed to the give and take that marriage involves." Ida herself had always been a take-charge girl, accustomed to getting her way. Stubbornness was an issue in their marriage, along with Ida's being a bigger star than Howard.

Ida and Howard starred together in the CBS comedy *Mr. Adams and Eve* (1957-58), portraying two movie stars who are married to each other. *Mr. Adams and Eve* is the everyday story of a movie-star couple living in Beverly Hills.

"I wanted the show to have a ring of truth to it, and exaggerated slightly for comedy."

The result was a hilarious and stylish sitcom, a wonderful send-up of Hollywood life in the fifties.

"That golden era, darling, when women were all dolled up, even when they had no place to go," Ida laughs!

Ida was nominated for two Emmy Awards for Best Actress in a Comedy Series. Unfortunately, she lost.

"I was just happy to be nominated, not once, but twice."

Just months after the filming of *Mr. Adams and Eve* ended, Universal developed a pilot for a possible half-hour drama starring Ida and Howard, along with silent film star Ramon Navarro, entitled *The Green Peacock*. This pilot never sold.

Ida in *Mr. Adams and Eve*

Emmy Nominees Ida Lupino, Ann Davis and Vivian Vance

On the set of *The Green Peacock*

13
The Bigamist

The Bigamist
A Filmakers Production Directed by Ida Lupino
Written by Larry Marcus and Lou Schor
Starring Ida Lupino, Joan Fontaine and Edmond O'Brien

Plot: Harry and Eve Graham want to adopt a child. Mr. Jordan, the adoption agent, investigates them, and discovers that Harry has a second wife. When he is about to call the police, Harry explains to him how he got involved with his second wife and how he got to be in the trouble that he is in.

In June of 1953, *The Bigamist* went before cameras and into the newspapers. This theme raised eyebrows in 1953, especially since there was an unusual relationship among the producer, director and the stars. Collier Young cast his wife, Joan Fontaine, in the film directed by his former wife, Ida Lupino. Edmond O'Brien played the bigamist,

"BIGAMIST" BIG BIG BOX BOX OFFICE!

The Critics Say—

"...Ida Lupino's performance (and directing) in 'The Bigamist' will get an Oscar!"
WALTER WINCHELL

"...A solid 'sleeper'- a hit that should have the gals dabbing at their eyes...It has all the elements without being melodramatic!"
JIMMY STARR
L. A. Herald-Express

And the *Public* says it with *DOLLARS*$!

JOAN FONTAINE · EDMOND O'BRIEN · IDA LUPINO
in **"THE BIGAMIST"** and EDMUND GWENN
Written for the screen and Produced by COLLIER YOUNG · Directed by IDA LUPINO
Distributed by Filmakers Releasing Organization

Get Set, New York!
EASTERN PREMIERE, ASTOR THEATRE ON BROADWAY OPENING CHRISTMAS NIGHT FOR EXTENDED RUN!

and Ida Lupino and Joan Fontaine were his wives. Collier talked his mother-in-law, Lillian Fontaine, into making a cameo appearance.

Collier's script, based on a story by Larry Marcus and Lou Shor, was a social drama about a man who makes a tragic mistake. Ida brings rare compassion to the situation, to the two woman played by herself and Joan Fontaine, and even to the man.

"After the divorce, Ida and I decided to stay in business. Our company was a good thing, since our divorce, the quality of our films have actually improved," Collier Young stated in an interview.

The lead actresses created vivid characters with different personalities that appeal to their shared husband. Joan Fontaine played

On the set of *The Bigamist* Collier, Joan and Ida.

a distant, career-oriented wife who works for a refrigeration company. Ida Lupino portrayed a waitress in a Chinese restaurant.

Ida used two different cameramen to shoot separate scenes of the female protagonists. Each cameraman used a subtly opposite style and highlighting lenses as laid down by Ida, the director, to visually portray each woman subjectively for the audience.

Though a small-budget picture, the cast had three Academy Award winners: Joan Fontaine for *Suspicion*, Edmund Gwenn for the Christmas classic *Miracle on 34th Street*, and Jane Darwell for *The Grapes of Wrath*.

Collier Young talked the cast into accepting "a participation deal," with profits from the grosses after the costs had been paid. Collier makes an appearance, sitting at the bar of the Chinese restaurant where Ida waited tables.

Ida Lupino became the first woman to direct herself in a major motion picture.

"It was difficult for me to determine the quality of my performance, so I relied on Collie. I had always sworn I would never do this. It is a new experience telling myself what to do. I am the one who wants and needs direction, but I never in the world expected to be doing this myself. I think it is the toughest thing I have ever attempted in my career. Collie would signal to me when I was doing something I would not like.

"To reduce production costs, Collier Young featured Cadillac, Coca Cola and United Airlines for revenue. Scenes were also shot in MacArthur Park and Chinatown, rather than on rental lots. I was acutely conscious of budget restraints and was careful to plan each scene to avoid costly technical mistakes."

Collier Young convinced Ida that they should distribute their own pictures.

"The greater the risk, the bigger the profits, Collie felt," Ida said.

The Bigamist opened to mixed reviews. Some thought that the ending was weak and lacked resolution. Ida liked the ending, in which the judge suspended the verdict until a later time.

"I wanted the audience to have the opportunity to resolve the issue in their own minds."

The New York Times hailed Ida, "This fragile director keels the action with such mounting tension, muted compassion and shark-like alacrity for behavior. The average spectator may feel they are eavesdropping on the excellent dialogue."

Ida Lupino once again received critical acclaim.

The Bigamist profits were low because of the self-distribution costs, but Collier Young insisted that the profits would eventually emerge. Sadly, they never did.

"I never got paid!" - Joan Fontaine

He's waiting...
just waiting
...to thumb
another
victim
down
the road
to death!

There he stands
...waiting to
add to America's
list of highway
atrocities! His
story screams
with thrills...
it rings with truth!

THE FILMAKERS PRESENT

The Hitch-Hiker

starring **EDMOND O'BRIEN**

FRANK LOVEJOY · WILLIAM TALMAN

Produced by   Directed by   Screenplay by
COLLIER YOUNG · IDA LUPINO · COLLIER YOUNG and IDA LUPINO

14
The Hitch-Hiker

From the Ida Lupino FBI File:
Released under the Freedom of Information Act

> FBI FILE: September 18, 1952 TELETYPE
> RKO STUDIOS DASH RESEARCH MATTERS.
> ATTION ASSISTANT DIRECTOR NICHOLS,
> WILLIAM FEEDER, DIRECTOR, PUBLIC
> RELATIONS, IDA LUPINO ACTRESS AND
> PRODUCER LEWIS RACHMILL, DIRECTOR, ALL
> RKO, ADVISED NINE SEVENTEEN LAST THAT
> RKO HAS IN PRODUCTION A FICTIONAL FILM
> ENTITLED 'THE DIFFERENCE' PRODUCED BY
> LUPINO, THAT RKO HAS IN PRODUCTION BY
> LUPINO, THAT THIS FILM WAS ORIGINALLY
> ENTITLED "THE DIFFERENCE" PRODUCED BY
> LUPINO, THAT THIS FILM WAS CONSIDERED
> AS A DOCUMENTARY ENTITLED "THE COOK

STORY" BASED ON THE CASE OF WILLIAM EDWARD COOK, JR., REBUFILE EIGHTYEIGHT DASH FIVE EIGHT SIX NINE, LA FILE EIGHTY EIGHT DASH ONE TWO SEVEN NINE, THAT CURRENT PRODUCTION SOMEWHAT PARALLELS ACTIVITIES OF COOK BUT DOES NOT IDENTIFY AS SUCH. ABOVE DESIRED TO KNOW IF FBI HAD JURISDICTION IN COOK CASE, ALSO DESIRED TO KNOW WHAT PROCEDURE FBI AGENTS USED IN QUESTIONING CERTAIN INDIVIDUALS DURING INVESTIGATION OF SIMILAR CASES, WHETHER OR NOT AGENTS COOPERATED CLOSELY WITH LOCAL POLI CE CASES THIS TYPE SO THAT THE FILM COULD BE AUTHENTIC AND NO OFFENSE CREATED IN INCORRECT PORTRAYAL OF FBI AGENTS. QUESTIONS ASKED WHETHER FBI WOULD

END PAGE ONE INDEXED-153 53 OCT 3-1952

TELETYPE
PAGE TWO

EXAMINE SCRIPTS AND OFFER SUGGESTIONS. ALL ABOVE WERE ADVISED OF BUREAU POLICY THAT ANY REQUESTS THIS SORT SHOULD BE REFERRED TO BUREAU DIRECT. NO COMMITMENTS MADE THIS OFFICE AND ONLY INFORMATION FURNISHED WAS GENERAL INFORMATION RELATING TO FBI JURISDCITION IN KIDNAPPING AND UFAP

CASES. MR. FEEDER ADVISED THAT BUREAU HAD BEEN CONTACTED IN APRIL, FIFTY TWO BY MR. J.B. BRECHEEN, BRANCH MANAGER, RKO, DISTRIBUTING AGENCY. WASHINGTON D.C. RE USE OF CERTAIN NAMES TO BE GIVEN AGENTS IN PICTURE. FEEDER ALSO ADVISED THAT IT WAS POSSIBLE THAT ACTORS USED IN FILM MIGHT NOT BE IDENTIFIED SPECIFICALLY AS FBI AGENTS BUT ONLY AS FEDERAL AGENTS. THAT IF ACTORS WERE PORTRAYED AS FBI AGENTS THAT IT WOULD BE POSSIBLE THAT HE WOULD HAVE RKO REPRESENTATIVE CONTACT BUREAU PERSONALLY IN WASHINGTON OR THAT HE HIMSELF MIGHT PHONE ASSISTANT NICHOLS DIRECT. FEEDER STATES THAT SHOOTING ON THIS PORTION OF THE PICTURE SCHEDULED WITHIN NEXT TEN DAYS FOR INFORMATION.

Carson END
LA R 9 WA DBD ALSO REPLAY

In California, 1950, Billy Cook murdered a family of five and a traveling salesman. He then kidnapped two prospectors, James Burke and Forrest Damron, who were on a hunting trip, and took them across the Mexican border to Santa Rosalia. There, Billy planned to kill them as well. The Mexican Police captured Billy Cook before he could carry out his plan. Police Chief Francisco Morales simply walked up to Billy and took his .32 revolver from him. Cook was arrested and extradited back to the United States, where he was handed over to FBI agents. He was tried and convicted in California. Billy Cook was put to death in the gas chamber of San Quentin Prison on December 12, 1952. He was 23 years old.

Ida Lupino had gone to see Billy Cook before he was executed.

"I wanted to see him and tell him I was making a film about him. With special permission from my buddies at the FBI, I entered San Quentin under strict security. I was allowed to see Billy Cook briefly for safety issues. I found San Quentin to be cold, dark and a very scary place inside. In fact, I was told by Collie (Collier Young) that I should not go; it was not safe. I wanted a release from Billy Cook to do our film. Billy Cook granted me the release that I needed to make our movie about him. I found him to be cold, calculating, and I was afraid of him. Billy Cook had 'Hard Luck' tattooed on the fingers of his left hand and a deformed right eyelid that would never close completely! I could not wait to get the hell out of San Quentin!"

Why would Ida Lupino make such a movie?

"I had gone to Palm Springs to receive an award from the Foreign Press Association for *Woman of the Year*. While I was in Palm Springs I interviewed Forrest Damron, one of the two hunters who had been abducted and held prisoner by Billy Cook in Baja.

Upon her return, Ida's film company, Filmakers, released a statement announcing their plans to do a picture based on the frightening experience of the kidnapped hunters.

The same day the release was made public, Geoffrey Shurlock of the Motion Picture Association telephoned Ida's office with strong objections to the making of this film. The Production Code prohibited screen depictions of contemporary notorious criminals. Filmakers went forward anyway, informing the papers that film rights had been obtained not only from the kidnapped victims, but from William (Billy) Cook, Jr. himself.

More trouble for Ida. In March, James V. Bennett, an official with the U.S. Bureau of Prisons, sent an angry letter to Joseph Breen about the "under handed trick" of obtaining William Cook's release for the picture. He urged the Motion Picture Association to withhold approval. Ida and Collier defended their actions. In a letter to Bennett they stated that they paid Cook's attorney three thousand dollars for a "valid and legal release." In addition, there would be no blood shed in the film.

Filmakers was an independent film company, specializing in documentary-style films, dealing with facts. They could produce pictures of greater importance and impact by bringing power and excitement to the screen. The U.S. Bureau of Prisons and the Motion Picture Association still would not allow a film based on the murders of William Cook. "No picture shall be dealing with the life of a notorious criminal of current or recent time which uses the name, nick name or alias of such."

Filmakers had no choice but to fictionalize the story and delete all references to William Cook, greatly changing the story and making the plot predictable.

The Hitch-Hiker went into production on June 24, 1952, and finished production in July. Location shooting took place in the Alabama Hills near Lone Pine and Big Pine, California.

THE HITCH-HIKER (1953)

Film Introduction:
"This is the true story of a man and a gun and a car. The gun belonged to the man. The car might have been yours or that young couple across

the aisle. What you will see in the next seventy minutes could have happened to you. For the facts are actual."

This film noir was directed by Ida Lupino, who was dressed in dungarees, sneakers and a check flannel shirt, topped with a baseball cap and tied-back hair. Trash cans full of soda pop on ice along with the bulky, industry standard 35mm Mitchell camera, are evidence that this film was shot under extremely difficult circumstances.

The screenplay written by Robert Joseph is about two fishing buddies who pick up a mysterious hitchhiker during a trip to Mexico. Ida and Collier Young produced this film. The plot was based on the story of *Out of the Past,* written by screenwriter Daniel Mainwaring, who was blacklisted at the time and did not receive screen credit. Ida took this and did a complete re-write.

Ida and Collier based their film screenplay on the true story of William Edward Cook, Jr., the psychopathic murderer. This film is considered to be the first film noir directed by a woman. The director of photography was RKO Pictures regular Nicholas Musuraca. RKO Pictures did distribute the picture, but it was Ida Lupino's film company, Filmakers, which produced it.

The film starred Edmond O'Brien, Frank Lovejoy and William Talman. These two men, O'Brien and Lovejoy, on a fishing trip pick up a hitch-hiker named Emmett Myers. William Talman portrayed Emmett Myers, who turns out to be a psychopath and has committed multiple murders.

Cameo appearances in *The Hitch-Hiker* included Clark Howat as the government agent, and Collier Young himself appeared as a Mexican peasant.

The Hitch-Hiker premiered in Boston on March 20, 1953, running seventy-one minutes in length. The film immediately went into general release. It was marketed with the tagline, "When was the last time you invited death into your car?"

WHY WE MADE "THE HITCH-HIKER"

BY COLLIER YOUNG AND IDA LUPINO

Once in a long while life itself turns up story material more exciting, more real and urgent than fiction. Such material started us on *THE HITCH-HIKER*.

But before we put it into production we asked ourselves:

Will it make a GOOD picture?

Will it make people want to see it?

Can it be exploited for extra box-office returns?

THE HITCH-HIKER provided a YES answer to all three questions.

The deeper we delved into the subject, the more excited we became. We were dealing with real people caught in one of the most dramatic adventures of our times. The basic theme was the question—in a race against death, which survives? The sane or the criminal mind? The answer provides the strange, driving suspense of *THE HITCH-HIKER*.

As we proceeded, daily newspaper headlines proved over and over again that we had drama and excitement and reality in our subject. They also convinced us that we had a film which could be effectively exploited by smart showmen everywhere.

Thanks to this and the brilliant starring performances by Edmond O'Brien, Frank Lovejoy and William Talman, we think you'll remember the 70 minutes of *THE HITCH-HIKER* for a long time.

COLLIER YOUNG   IDA LUPINO

The *New York Times* gave *The Hitch-Hiker* a mixed review in its initial release. The acting, direction, and use of locations were praised, but the plot was deemed to be predictable. Ida Lupino stated, "It was based on a true story. Did the critics think there should be some plot twist? I wanted realism! To appease the censors at the Hays Office, I reduced the number of deaths to three!"

Critic John Krewson lauded the work of Ida Lupino and wrote, "As a screen writer and director, Lupino has an eye for the emotional truth hidden within the taboo or mundane...in *The Hitch-Hiker*, arguably Lupino's best film and the only true Noir directed by a woman...in addition to her critical but compassionate sensibility, Lupino had a great filmmaker's eye, using gorgeous, ever-present loneliness of empty highways in *The Hitch-Hiker* to set her characters apart."

Time Out Film Guide wrote of the film, "Absolutely assured in her creation of the bleak, noir atmosphere—whether in the claustrophobic confines of the car or lost in the arid expanses of the desert—Lupino never relaxes the tension for one moment. Yet her sensitivity is also up front; charting the changes in the men's relationship as they bicker about how to deal with their captor, stressing that only through friendship can they survive. Taut, tough, and entirely without much glorification, it's a gem with first class performances from its three protagonists, deftly characterized without resort to cliché."

Film critic Dennis Schwartz wrote of the film, "It is pleasure to watch the action unfold without resorting to clichés. Talman's performance as a sadistic sleaze was powerful. His random crime spree strikes at the heart of the middle-class American's insecurity about there being no place free of crime."

William Talman later went on to portray Hamilton Burger, the opposing council in the television series classic, *Perry Mason*. His character only won one case against the famed attorney, on a technicality. Barbara Hale (Della Street in the *Perry Mason* television series) said, "I was always grateful to Ida for giving him his big break!"

In 1998, *The Hitch-Hiker* was selected for preservation in the United States National Film Registry as being "culturally, historically and aesthetically significant." The restoration of this classic film noir was overseen by renowned film director, Louis Antonelli.

Ida on set reviewing her shooting script fot *The Hitch-Hiker*

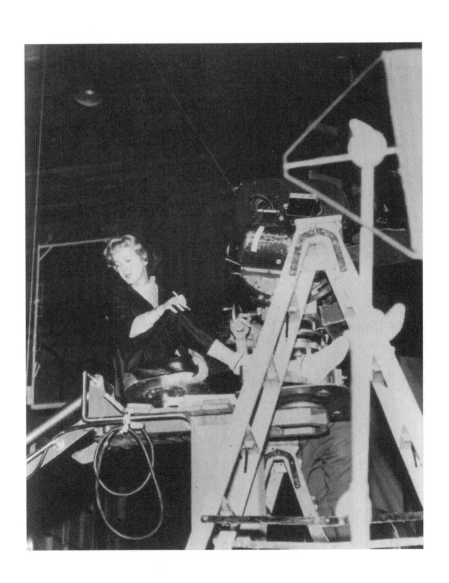

15
Me, Mother Directress

IDA HAD BRANCHED OUT into film directing and producing in 1949, becoming one of two women to enter the still male-dominated field. The first was Dorothy Arzner. Ida was the second woman admitted into The Director's Guild of America, better known as the DGA. She was known as the darling of the "Tough Guy" school of directing, along with some of her favorites, Raoul Walsh, Fritz Lang and William Wellman. Actors and crews adored Ida.

When I asked Ida about being one of Hollywood's first female directors, she replied, "I didn't see myself as any advance guard or feminist. I had to do something to fill up my time. For about eighteen months in the mid-forties, I could not get a job as an actress in pictures; along with Annie Sheridan, Humphrey Bogart and John Garfield. I was on suspension from Warner Bros. It seems we were always on suspension. When you turned down something you were suspended. I don't know if it was Jack Warner or who it was. I was the only one who had a radio clause in my contract, so I was able to keep alive as a radio actress. I was working every solitary week doing radio, Silver Theater with Boyer on his show, with Tyrone Power and C. B. De Mille on his Lux Theatre."

"When I did work at Warner's, I was bored to tears with standing around the set while someone else seemed to do all the interesting work. I teamed up with my then-husband Collier Young and formed my own production company, The Filmakers. We chose controversial, socially conscious issues for themes of our movies: rape, bigamy, polio, and unwed motherhood. We co-wrote a screenplay called *Not Wanted* and put it before the cameras."

According to film scholar Richard Koszarski, "Her films display the obsessions and consistencies of a true Auteur. What is most interesting about her films are not her stories on unwed motherhood or the tribulations of career women, but the way she uses male actors, particularly in *The Bigamist* and *The Hitch-Hiker* (both 1953). Lupino was able to reduce the male to the same sort of dangerous, irrational force that women represented in the most male-directed examples of Hollywood Film Noir." Later these were dubbed "Lupino Noir."

"Those were thrilling days for us. We co-wrote and co-produced, and I went on to direct each successive film. We discovered new talent, and we did the kind of film that is 'new wave' today. We took topics that were pretty daring at the time. We would shoot these films in about thirteen days and at a budget of less than two hundred thousand dollars, and they were 'A' pictures."

After the demise of her film company in 1954, Ida was in great demand for directing television and building a sterling reputation as one of television's top directors. She directed such programs as *Alfred Hitchcock Presents*.

"I would rather direct an episode of *Alfred Hitchcock Presents* for $5,000.00 than to star in one for $25,000.00. Directing is so much eas ier than acting. The actor deals with false emotion, produced on cue. The director has problems but they are all normal. He doesn't

On the set with Alfred Hitchcock

Ida and Ronald Reagan

have to smile into the camera while suffering through with any early morning grouch."

"I also directed *General Electric Theatre*, starring Ronald Reagan. Ronnie never knew his lines. I had to send him back to his dressing room to learn them. If he did not learn them, I would direct him with his back to the camera. I had to feed him his lines!"

Ida on the set stated to the cast and crew, "God help us all if Ron is ever elected President of the United States!"

"Keeping a feminine approach is vital; men hate bossy females. You do not tell a man; you suggest to him. 'Darlings, Mother has a problem. I'd love to do this. Can you do it?' It sounds kooky, I know. But can you do this for Mother? And, they do it. That way I got more cooperation. I tried to never blow up. A woman cannot afford to do that. They're waiting for it. With the exception of one or two pills I've met along the line, most of the crews I've worked with have been wonderful. As long as you keep your temper, the crew will go along with you. I loved being called Mother.

"If I get a script in time, I prepare on a week-end. I go out on the back lot or to the sets on Saturday and Sunday, when it is nice and quiet, and map out my set-ups. I do that every time it's at all possible. I went out on the back lot at Universal a while back to prepare an episode of *The Virginian*, but I had forgotten those studio tours. You know, twelve thousand people traipsing all over the place over the weekend. There I was on the set, dripping wet in the killing heat, wearing no makeup, looking like a witch searching for a house to haunt, and these tours started coming through.

"The bright young know-it-all guide would tell his eager charges, 'And there, ladies and gentlemen, is the famous director Ida Lupino preparing for *The Virginian*.' I tell you I wanted to die. I was in dire need of a friend and, luckily, I found one, a studio policeman. He sympathized with my need to work in peace and anonymity, and so he'd keep track of the tour trams, and when one was headed my way he'd rush over and like a latter day Paul Revere signal, 'The tourists are coming.' Then I would duck behind a building and hide."

Norman MacDonnell, longtime producer of "Gunsmoke," said of Ida Lupino, "You used Ida when you had a story about a woman with some dimension, and you really wanted it hard hitting."

While her feature films were primarily aimed at female audiences, on television Ida quickly became known for her skill at directing westerns, mysteries, detective dramas — shows aimed at the male viewer, and many featuring all male casts.

"Lovey bird, you've been shot in the belly. You must suffer, darling!"

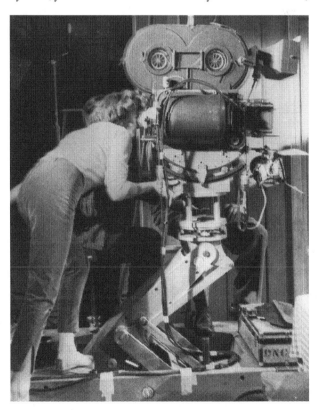

Ida directing. Credit: Associate Press

"This is one of my favorite articles written about me, wearing velvet pants."

TV Guide, January 24-30, 1959 – "Bring In The Nervous Poodle"
Ida Lupino in velvet pants, creates new lingo as she directs a Western.

Ida Lupino may never tame the West but when she directed a *Have Gun Will Travel* episode, she did her level best to tranquilize it. In a single day of shooting, Ida Lupino made obsolete every Western studio cliché used in Hollywood since William S. Hart rode the celluloid range.

Instead of puttees, Miss Lupino wore velvet pants. Instead of a riding crop, she brandished a lipstick. And, when, she wanted a wrangler to keep a tight reign on his horse, she said, "Dahling, please hold the poodle-dog's leash."

In a scene where she wanted a horse to shy, Miss Lupino told the assistant director, "Baby, let's bring in a nervous poodle here." She referred to star Richard Boone as "Dicky Bird" and to the villain as "Lovey."

At one point, Miss Lupino was heard to say, "Cut. Printsville. How does it look?"

Translation: "End of scene. Print it. How does it look?"

"And, another favorite of mine, Darling!"

TV Guide, October 8-14, 1966 – "Ida Lupino, Director," by Dwight Whitney
Follow Me Mother, Here We Go, Kiddies!

118

Excerpt: Ida Lupino, a 'little old ex-limey broad,' Directs
the most rip-roaring episodes on TV

It's been a tough couple of days for Mother. The
temperature at the Iverson's Ranch, 16,000 dust washed
acres of gully and mustard seed some 25 miles northwest of
Hollywood, hovers around 90 degrees. Yesterday the crew
killed two rattlesnakes and a tarantula. Today bees and the
red ants have taken over. They buzz the portable dressing
rooms, the bank of chemical toilets, the prop trucks, the
catering wagon, the 14 head of horses, the wranglers, the
stuntmen, script girl, grips, actors, press agents. It is the
last day of location shooting of a *Virginian* script called
"Deadeye Dick" and Mother is several pages behind.

This morning an ingénue took an unscheduled saddle
fall and cracked a vertebra. The wild heifer got away and
held up shooting an hour. One of the key horses in a chase
sequence pulled up lame. Then-damn-it began to rain when
everybody knows it never rains at this time of year. Still
Mother is all aplomb, which is not easy for a girl with the
dust of Iverson's sifting down over her. She doesn't need her
dainty apple green collapsible stool (the one with "Mother"
painted on it) or her matching bullhorn.

"Any rocks up there to give you a problem, Darling?"
she is saying. "Now, Walter, baby, while we're here we might
as well take the posse through. I want my camera here.
That's right. You read my mind, love. Now, the posse won't
be coming through at such a clip. Start out at a reasonable
speed. That's it, sweetheart. Now we are lathering the horses
in this sequence, sweetie? If not we should be."

A prop man appears with an aerosol can of men's

shaving cream and begins slapping it on the flanks of the horses. "That's divine, love. Ok, follow Mother; here we go, kiddies!" "Mother" is Ida Lupino, the first and maybe the last of the lady TV directors.

Still she keeps on directing, even when producers call her up and tell her, "Ides, baby, I've got a tender little story I want you to do.

"Of course, I know exactly what he means, sweetie," she explains. "He means he got a runaway horse, two shoot-outs and a cattle stampede he wants me to handle. So I take the job, what else?

"No one has asked me to direct a love story!"

Ida adds to this article, "Any woman who wishes to smash into the world of men isn't very feminine. I retained every feminine trait while directing. Men prefer it that way. They're more co-operative if they see that fundamentally you are of the weaker sex, even though you are in the position to give orders, which normally is the male prerogative, or so he likes to think, any way. At times, I pretended to a cameraman to know less than I do. That way I got more cooperation.

"Darling, while I have encountered some resentment from the male species for intruding into their world, I give them no opportunity to think I've stayed where I don't belong. I assume no masculine characteristics which can be a fault of a career woman rubbing shoulders with their male counter parts, who become arrogant or authoritative.

"I would love to see more women working as directors and producers!"

Time Magazine, Friday, February 8, 1963 –
"Mother Lupino"

Big Augie sits in the meat cooler. Augie is so sweaty

that on a warm day the cooler is the only place he can keep his body heat down. In comes one of his hoods, to report a botched heist. Augie pulls a wicket knife, slams the hood against a meat hook and threatens to make him look like a slab of Grade 'A' Prime.

A woman in pink slacks, straw hat and cowboy boots interrupts, "Peter, darling," she husks, "Hold the knife this way and make sure we see that sweet meat hook."

This well-chilled slab of sadism occurs in a forthcoming scene in *The Untouchables*.

The Lucrezia Borgia in boots is familiar to middle-aging movie fans as the tough-kitten, been around blonde (sometimes brunette) of several dozen B pictures and several A's. To the cast of *The Untouchables*, she is an A-plus director. Her name? Ida Lupino.

The Untouchables' Robert Stack (Elliott Ness) attributes her success to the fact that as an actress "she knows when something would feel uncomfortable on a performer." She is also famed for her 'glue.' Her ability to link scenes together smoothly, as when the distorted image of a gangster in a fun house mirror gives way in the blink of an eye to a beautiful girl looking in mirror in a fur wrap.

Ida rules more by sex appeal than by fiat. "Can we try it this way, darling?" she would murmur, "Or would you hate me for that, sweetheart?" Or as she adjusts the welder's mask, designed to protect her from flying chips and plaster, "Darling, could you hold the gun this way and shoot down the alley? Try it, sweetheart, and see if it works."

The actors affectionately call her "Mother."

Ida Lupino's Director's Chair reads "Mother of All of Us."

Credit: The Louis Antonelli Collection

Ida reviewing her shooting script for "The Masks." She was the only
woman ever to direct a *Twilight Zone*; or to act in one and direct one!

On the set of *Gilligan's Island*. Ida directed a total of five episodes;
two with credits - three without.

Ida directing Ronald Reagan in *GE Theatre*

16
The First Meeting

I FIRST MET IDA LUPINO on February 4, 1983. It was her sixty-fifth birthday. I was working with Cara Lund of the Lund Agency at the time, as her sub-agent. Cara knew Ida and told me it was her birthday. I thought we should send her some flowers. Cara said I should take them to Ida personally, so I did.

I drove out to Brentwood Heights and parked out on the street in front of her home, which was surrounded by large iron gates. I didn't expect her to be outside in her front yard, gardening. As soon as I stepped out of my car, I heard a great dramatic voice project, "If you don't move that car, it is going to get awfully damn wet!"

Ida was watering her lawn. I couldn't see her too well because of all of the overgrown foliage that constituted a large wall of hedge.

I replied, "Ida dear, I have some flowers for you."

"Are you from the florist?" she asked.

"No!"

"Is there a bomb in them?"

"No!"

"If you like them, you keep them!"

"No! They are for you!"

"Can't you say anything else but 'no'?"

"No!"

Ida began to laugh and so did I. She later told me that I reminded her of a television commercial.

Her voice changed direction. This time it was coming from the other side of her enormous property. I walked over that way. There Ida Lupino appeared, walking down a path which leads to her driveway. Ida was dressed like a bag lady; wearing a big old coat, baggy pants with a shawl draped over her head. She loved that term, and laughed every time she heard it. Ida was carrying a lot of keys. She was repeating our conversation, like she was doing a scene from a commercial, and continued to laugh.

Ida walked up to the gate and unlocked this long bicycle lock, the kind that locks bicycle spokes but with a small key. "You really do have flowers for me," she uttered in a much softer tone of voice.

I said, "Yes!"

A little tear came to those large pale blue eyes of hers when she took the flowers, placing her hand on mine, and said, "Thank you, dear!"

I told her that I had always admired her and her work.

I remembered her vividly as Dr. Cassandra in *Batman*, from when I was a child.

She said, "Thank you, and God bless you."

I got back in my car and drove to the Valley, thinking what a lonely lady she must be, living out there all by herself. I called Cara and told her what had happened. She was pleased and thought I could help Ida Lupino.

Once home, I ran into my mother, Emily McLaughlin Hunter, who portrayed nurse Jessie Brewer on the ABC daytime serial *General Hospital,* since April 1, 1963, and with whom I was living at the time.

She asked me where I had been. I told her.

She said, "Ida Lupino's birthday – she's one of the greats. Send her a candy clown from Arthur Finley's." Emily sends them to everybody on their birthdays. I said, "How about a candy cat? She loves cats." Emily wasn't feeling very well at the time and went back to bed.

I called Ida to let her know about the delivery because of her gates. She told me the baby roses were the most beautiful flowers she had ever received and she had just given them some water. Ida said she would keep a lookout for the delivery and that she would call me later.

Well, an hour later my phone rang. "Is this Mary Ann?" I heard that great voice again. "This is Ida Lupino. A very nice man, who recognized me, handed me a blue candy cat with balloons. How did you know I love cats and that he matches my hallway? I just love him. I had a candy, too. Thank your Mum, too!" Ida articulates her words very well and has a slight British accent. "I used to watch her on General Hospital." Ida loves to talk!

"The next time you come, you'll have to meet my cat, 'Timothy O'Shea.' He's a brown and white Persian." She added, "I have to get ready for my birthday party that my sister is giving for me. My police captain, Tim O'Sullivan, is taking me." I later found out he was retired security officer and paid by her sister, Rita, to take her out.

Then Ida added, "I want you to come up and have tea with me on Monday at 1:00 p.m."

I was surprised by her invitation and told Ida I would see her then. I was excited and thrilled to go visit her, but a little uneasy. Cara had told me about the poor condition of Ida's home.

17
The Christmas House

On February 7, 1983, precisely at 1:00 pm, I arrived at Brentwood Heights for the second time. This time, there was no great voice telling me to move my car because it would get wet.

I pulled in front of Ida's double gate and sounded my horn four times, as instructed. Ida had called me Sunday night to tell me about a film that was on television that she thought I might like to watch. During that conversation, she told me about her codes: four rings— hang up, four rings— hang up, etc., until she answered her phone. The same code existed for a car horn, four beeps of a car horn for her to open her gates. At that time, she also told me she had plumbing problems. She had two buckets…one for her and one for guests.

At five minutes past, Ida appeared at her gate and unlocked it. This time she was all dressed up, wearing a bronze colored satin blouse, black slacks and black silk scarf, black shoes and a bright red wig, Lucille Ball red!

I took Ida a bottle of champagne. We walked around back. Ida's house faced the back of her property, and the pool was in front. As we walked through her yard, I noticed that everything was overgrown, like in the film classic *Sunset Blvd.* Ida's pool looked like the Loch Ness Monster had lived there but died in it! What's more, there was furniture in it—patio furniture, and years of dark green slime and scum.

Ida's ranch-style front porch was all decorated for Christmas and, under all the years of decorations, it looked like at one time it was white, but now it was dingy and grey. She said, "You must think I'm awfully eccentric with all these Christmas decorations but my police captain won't let me take them down. They cheer him up when he's depressed. So, if people think I'm eccentric, it's damn well too bad!"

Ida would later tell me these decorations were a memorial tribute to Connie Lupino and Collier Young, who both died on Christmas.

We walked inside and there was the "candy cat" in her entry way, and it did match her walls. Immediately inside, Ida locked the door.

"You can't be too careful around here. My neighbors are just awful!" Ida told me about all of her paintings and antiques, which had several years of dust on them. Most of them, she explained, were purchased in Santa Barbara, one of her favorite places. She added that she had filmed *Jennifer* there with Duff. If you mention his name to her she replies, "Howard, who?"

As I walked through the house, I noticed that the walls were plaster and cracking; there were taped-on picture cards of cats and dogs. Each picture had a bow taped to it. Ida had given them all names, and had funny sayings for them. These were her friends.

The house was enormous. It was Early American, all done in blues and pinks.

Everything looked so old and depressing. I could understand why Ida had bows on the walls and left her Christmas decorations up for seven years. It wasn't her police captain who got depressed; it was Ida. Considering her situation, however, Ida had a lot to be depressed about—her three failed marriages, her waning career, her fading looks, money worries, and her wrecked house.

We ended up in the den, where we drank champagne and chatted for eight hours. Ida did most of the talking!

Bogie and Ida personally inscribed by Ida.

"I haven't had champagne in years, and Ida, you talk too much!"

I found her to be very direct and outspoken. She told me, right up front, that she wasn't an alcoholic, drug addict, or a lesbian, and that she didn't trust women.

"I don't like to see woman behaving in a masculine manner. I'm not a woman's woman. I'm not a group type."

So, what was I doing there, I thought to myself.

Ida added, "I prayed to God that He would send someone to help me, and here you are!"

She talked about her favorite movies that she made—*Ladies in Retirement* and *Road House*—and about her favorite leading men— "Bogie" and Robert Ryan.

"I can only tell you, I loved Bogie! Yes and I think he loved me. I guess he didn't find me too bad. I think it could have been a going-going romance, but it didn't turn out for us to be lovers."

I told Ida how much I enjoyed her in the ABC Movie of the Week, *Woman In Chains* (1972), in which she portrays a sadistic warden called Claire Tyson in a women's prison. I recited for Ida two of her great lines, "My girls are special. They help me run this block." Ida seemed very surprised!

"That is the one where they shoot me on the roof and I fall. I took a bad fall. I remember that. I played a horrible sadistic person! I am surprised you weren't afraid to come here!"

I laughed and replied, "No!" Ida smiled.

She told me about Duff and his being "queer as muck," an old British saying that she loves. Ida recalled the time she came home from directing and found Howard in the den, in a compromising position with their daughter Bridget's boyfriend.

Ida added that she was still married to Duff and spoke openly about their marriage.

"My marriage to Duff was all right up to a point but the laughter went out of it very early on. Howard and I had very few happy times. Several things that stand out in my mind were the celebrations, birthdays and anniversaries; they all seemed—forced to do."

Howard had left Ida for good in September 1972.

I found it sad that to learn Ida hadn't seen her daughter in two years. Her relationship with Bridget deteriorated after Howard left. Bridget lived in San Francisco and was practicing Zen Buddhism

The last time Ida saw her daughter, by accounts, was at her sister Rita's wedding, at the exclusive Mulholland Tennis Club in Beverly Hills, where Ida slapped her daughter across the face, not once but twice, for showing up with someone other than her husband, whom she had married some years before.

Later, I would try to help patch up things between Ida and Bridget. I took them out to dinner at The Cork Screw. We had gone to Hamburger Hamlet first. Ida was in a bad mood. She did not like our table, so she grabbed one of the chairs and threw it across the room.

I said jokingly, "Ida, now do you want to throw the table as well?" She replied, "No, darling I do not have time!"

At dinner, I had a conversation with Ida. I had a conversation with Bridget. Very few words were exchanged between them, and the building tension was unpleasant. Bridget casually calling her mother "Ida" did not help.

Ida could never erase from her memory the repulsive image of Bridget's boyfriend with Howard in their family den. This caused a tragic and irreparable rift between Ida and her daughter, with Ida furiously shouting at the time, "You love your father so much, look at this!"

Ida did see more of her sister, Rita. Although Ida and Rita loved each other, these Lupino girls had very strong personalities that often clashed. Dinners and holidays were often refereed by Rita's husband Gunter Seifer and me when the inevitable sparks flew. Gunter would take Ida and me out on his yacht with Ida, naturally, taking the helm. She was a great sailor. Ida had co-owned a boat named "The Bahia" many years ago with her dear friend, Sandy Perry.

As Ida continued to talk and reminisce, I noticed all the abruptly thrown garbage hidden in corners, under furniture and in other places. Also, the wildly overgrown lawn hadn't been cut in months, which added ominous foreshadowing of what I began to suspect. Ida's sharp, intuitive sense seemed to penetrate my thoughts as she added with a tinge of embarrassment, "My housekeeper, 'Ellie,' had to quit as she had several tumor operations."

Ida's former pool man ran off with her diamond necklace, and she loaned her car to a friend, who never bothered to bring it back. Ida added that the Westwood Village Plumbers ruined her house.

"They broke a pipe out in the lawn and it flooded the house. That's why all the bags of garbage are inside—to hold back the water."

I later learned that Ida owed Beverly Wilshire Rubbish Co. over $2,300.00, and they were preparing to put a hard lien on her property.

I told Ida that I knew of a great plumber, Paul. He could fix her plumbing and it wouldn't be expensive. She seemed overwhelmed and relieved by this offer and asked that I send him over anytime!

Ida stopped talking about herself and started asking me a lot of questions about my life. She told me I wasn't the agent type and that I seemed to be more business oriented. My dear, you are not mean enough to be an agent!" It was then that she told me about her business manager, Mr. David Martin, and how he "ripped her off."

We later had him audited by an accounting firm. We couldn't find any grounds for embezzlement, but he did mismanage her money.

I told her I was a part-time business manager for Emily McLaughlin Productions. Ida then asked me if I would be her business manager.

"You can have fifty percent—I'll put it in writing!" Ida stated. "Business Managers don't get fifty percent. They get five percent," I responded.

Our long, productive business and personal relationship began at that very moment; and what followed became an amazing adventure for over twelve irreplaceable years.

18

The Duchess of Dirt vs. the Queen of Phones

MY FIRST OF MANY PROJECTS was to install a telephone so Ida could have it right next to her. Her telephone was in the master bedroom, which she no longer could use. This room looked like a true-to-life tornado, named Howard, had struck it. FEMA could easily provide disaster training in this room. It took Ida quite some time to maneuver through the zigzag maze of discarded items to get to the phone. Her codes—four rings hang up, four rings hang up—gave Ida extra time to reach the ringing phone. I went and purchased a long telephone cord, along with a new telephone for Ida.

Her telephone jack was the older four-pin type, not the kind that you could just plug in a longer cord. I had to rewire the jack. Ida stood next to me, intensely watching everything I did. I was sitting on the floor, busy at work, connecting the black, red, yellow and green wires. She told me she could have used me on her sets doing wiring!

Ida stars in *The Twilight Zone*

Ida called me "The Queen of Phones" after her new telephone was installed. Ida's new telephone could now be next to her in her den, where she spent most of her time watching television and classic films, like the character she portrayed in *The Twilight Zone* episode "The Sixteen Millimeter Shrine." My friend, Wendy, would tease me that one day I would go to see Ida and she would have vanished into the television set, leaving her scarf behind as did her character, Barbara Jean Trenton, in this haunting episode written by Rod Serling.

Next, I sent Paul, the plumber from T & M Plumbing, to Ida's home. Paul and his crew cleaned out the main sewer line, which was backed up with solid sewage and tree roots. The bill was only a little over $200.00. I could tell Ida was having severe financial trouble, so I had pre-arranged to have the bill paid for her if it was high. Ida wrote out a check and was thrilled that her plumbing had been repaired.

My friend, John, started to clean her house. Ida introduced herself as "The Duchess of Dirt" when he arrived. We all laughed!

John started with Ida's bathroom off of the den. Within hours Ida had a clean and working bathroom. She was forever grateful! John continued to come and meticulously clean her enormous house when he was not attending college classes. Ida would pay him each time he came and wrote funny and grateful comments on the checks to him, such as "for a new brick floor with many bricks" or "for many hours of very hard work."

Steve, another friend of mine, joined our cleaning group. Steve and John were both very good looking and Ida thought of them as her "boys." She would call me "Annie" after her very dear friend, actress Ann Sheridan. One evening, Steve came to start work on Ida's swimming pool, to retrieve the furniture out of it that somehow found its way in there. Steve was sitting on the edge of the diving board, I was sitting behind him, holding on to him, and Ida was sitting behind me, holding on to me. Steve had a deep sea fishing pole, extra long and very strong. He would hook and reel in the pieces of the patio furniture that were in the pool.

Steve jokingly said, "Has anyone seen Howard Duff lately? Maybe he is in here too." Ida started laughing so hard, as did Steve and I, that we all almost ended up the pool.

Gary, my Mother's pool man, came and drained the enormous pool. He acid washed it and replaced the pool motor. Steve spent many weeks trimming all of the trees on her half-acre property and cutting Ida's lawn. For sometime John continued to clean and paint her house.

I would take Ida out for lunch. She especially liked Hamburger Hamlet in Brentwood. She loved their hamburgers with mushrooms.

Women in Chains. Warden Tyson. Written by Rita Lakin.

Mary Ann and Ida at charity event.

Another restaurant Ida liked was The Cork Screw. We would often see Dean Martin and his manager there having dinner. We would all sit together and talk.

Ida appeared at charity events in Brentwood for The Shelter for Battered Women, and she was a guest judge for the Brentwood Chili Cook Off. These events were arranged through the Brentwood Chamber of Commerce. During the event for The Shelter for Battered Women, Ida and I were confronted, at our table, by two paparazzi, and they snapped our photo. Ida purchased this photo for $175.00 in cash from these two men, who sold it to her out of their car. Ida captioned this photo, "Would you buy a use car from these two?"

Ida would also appear at meetings for The John Garfield Foundation. She had agreed to direct their production of their play

Witness for the Prosecution. The foundation held a fundraiser at the exclusive Riviera Tennis Club in Pacific Palisades, but John Garfield's brother, Mike, backed out of this production.

We would go shopping to purchase new carpet, wall paper and furnishings. I arranged the purchase and delivery of new household appliances, such as a stove, refrigerator, washer and dryer. I had to show Ida how to use the new stove. The washer and dryer were just pieces of furniture to her, something to put plants on.

Ida fired her business manger, David Martin, owner of Business Administration. Mr. Martin, only after a very stern letter from famed Beverly Hills attorney Simon Taub, returned a few shares of stock that Ida owned. These shares of stock were sold for $25,000.00. The funds from the sale of stock were used to pay for the restoration of Ida's home.

I obtained Ida's Social Security for her and her DGA (Director's Guild of America) pension. The DGA did not have records of Ida's early directorial efforts, so I had to find documentation to prove to the DGA that Ida in fact had directed so many and varied production segments. My efforts paid off for Ida when she received her Director's Guild monthly pension and a lump-sum payment. I purchased for Ida shares of stock, privately held, in Brentwood Square Savings. Ida loved to go into the bank, wearing her new mink coat and speak with all of the employees.

"You can all go home early, Darlings, I own the bank!"

When at Ida's former bank, Bank of America, she would go in, never wait in line but sit at the vice president's desk. If the phone was ringing and no one answered it, Ida would answer the phone.

"Hello Darling! This is Bank of America!"

Now with her Social Security benefits, DGA pension, and SAG (Screen Actor's Guild) pension, Ida's lifestyle improved, along with the condition of her home. "Our" home restoration project took over two years to be completed. The home was too large for Ida and full of bad memories.

"Annie, I want to get the hell out of this house and move. It has too many bad memories of Howard Duffel Bag." (Ida called Howard this because he was always leaving her.)

She tenderly added, "I want to live closer to you, Annie!"

There had been many issues over the years between Ida and her neighbors. Many a time, her next door neighbors received a shower from Ida and her garden hose. She liked to water her lawn and the neighbors. Not the neighbor's lawn—the neighbors!

One afternoon, I arrived to take Ida out shopping and to lunch. I entered through a gate on the side by Ida's neighbors, the ones she did not like. I usually did not come in that direction. Ida was watering her lawn. Unfortunately, she thought I was the neighbor that she did not like. Well, she blasted me with her hose. When Ida realized it was me, she tried to turn off the nozzle but she turned it the wrong way. I ran over to assist Ida with her hose, the water pressure built and we were both drenched.

"When you are all wet, you are all wet!" Ida stated, laughing!

It was a beautiful sunny day, so we stayed outside chatting until we dried off.

Ida's neighbors would also receive visits from an angry Ida when they would park in front of her house, the famous Lupino temper ever so present, and pitched.

"I have a very bad temper; I have always had it. I try to control it but there's this little devil in me that comes out at times."

Ida previously was on probation for 'malicious mischief' stemming from an incident with her neighbor's gardener's car. This car was parked out in front of Ida's home and was blocking her gate. Ida apparently hit the car repeatedly with her broom and this 'act' of hers damaged the car.

20
Farewell to Howard

IDA WISHED TO WORK WITH HOWARD as she did with her previous husbands, Louis Hayward (who acted opposite Lupino in *Ladies in Retirement*) and Collier Young (who wrote and produced films with her). "I have received so many great scripts, but I want Howard to play the lead!"

Little did studio people know that at home Howard was taking out his limited acting career on his wife with verbal threats and physical abuse.

Joan Fontaine, "Howard had no respect for Ida!"

Sam Goldwyn wanted Ida Lupino for several pictures, but lost interest in her because she was always promoting Howard, a decision Ida later regretted.

The Duffs went to Santa Barbara in early 1953 to film the mystery movie, *Jennifer*. This film starred Ida as a frightened caretaker of an enormous estate. The owner had vanished. Howard had a minor role as a grocer, and was second billed after his wife.

143

Jennifer candid rehearsal

Jennifer failed to capture audiences.

Howard Duff made headlines, weeks later, when he landed on the floor at the Villa Nova Restaurant on Sunset Boulevard. Reports were told that Duff became outraged after several drinks and began to threaten and demean everyone in the place. He tossed a cocktail glass and an ashtray. He bellowed threats, which caused the customers to leave the restaurant. At the end of the bar was Jack Buchtel, a prominent restaurant owner.

He tried to reason with Howard Duff. Duff took a swing, Buchtel sidestepped Howard's punch, and Howard landed on the floor!

It was reported that Ida ran up and tossed a glass of water in her husband's face. Howard struggled to get up and managed to throw a right punch again at Jack Buchtel. Jack again blocked Howard's punch and then threw a punch of his own, hitting Duff in the nose; and Howard was on the floor again. Ida ran over with another glass of water; this time she threw it in Jack's face. Jack Buchtel made his way out of the restaurant, with an enraged Ida Lupino following with another glass of water. An innocent bar patron began a fast walk down Sunset Boulevard with Ida Lupino close behind. Ida ran out of steam after a few blocks and returned to her half-conscious husband.

This incident made headlines: "Sunset Row at Dawn Features Ida Lupino's Mate."

Ida had stolen the spotlight from her brawling husband. Duff came to realize that he lived in the shadow of his famous wife. He was "Mr. Lupino," and did not like it at all!

Despite the clashes, something clicked with Ida and Howard on screen; but the Duffs' marital problems had become evident.

"Howard did not like being married. He felt trapped and was unable to tell his wife this. When pressures mounted, Howard would simply disappear, sometimes for weeks on end," commented Vincent Sherman.

While pondering yet another divorce, Ida and partners David Niven, Dick Powell and Charles Boyer formed *Four Star Playhouse*.

"Four Star had taken over the RKO-Pathe lot in Culver City. This lot was formerly the Selznick Studios, where *Gone With The Wind* had been filmed. I was impressed with the quality of Four Star Productions, and, on December 31, 1953, I made my debut on the small screen in 'House for Sale.' I portrayed a woman who encounters a psychopathic killer. I continued on, becoming their fourth star."

"Howard and I met to discuss our divorce, after being separated this time for three months. Surprisingly, we decided to give it another try!"

Howard must have needed the work, insider studio people thought.

In February, Ida returned to television for the *Ford Theatre*, starring in "The Marriageable Male," co-starring with Jack Lemon.

Ida and Howard appeared together in an episode of *The Dinah Shore Chevy Show*.

By April, the Duffs were estranged yet again, and no longer spoke with one another. They patched up their marriage long enough to do a show together, "Season to Love," directed by Ted Post. Ted Post could not understand Ida's preoccupation with the lighting.

Ida suggested, "Darling do not shoot me as if I was eighteen years old. We need some soft lenses or maybe a horse blanket," she joked.

Howard's calmness had melted, if indeed he ever had any. Once again, they planned a divorce. Howard found work in forgettable B-pictures.

Ida was selected to star in better pictures, and to direct one. Columbia Pictures hired Ida Lupino to direct *The Trouble with Angels*, starring Rosalind Russell as Mother Superior. This was Ida's big break at directing a feature film for a major studio.

Rosalind Russell recalled, "What I admire about Ida is that she comes to the set each morning fully prepared. She knows what she wants and she knows how to do it. Ida is clear, concise and has a great sense of humor.

Above all, Ida has vitality and enthusiasm. And we enjoy a good stiff drink together after a long day of shooting!"

"I knew Roz for years. I loved her. She was a wonderful woman and a magnificent human being. Rosalind was a joy to direct. She was the most talented actress and very, very helpful to others working with her. Roz gave one of her best performances ever."

"I eventually shot some good work by Hayley Mills, though she was very difficult to direct. Ann Harding was a delight. I was not asked to direct the sequel, but I was paid $25,000 to direct the original picture."

Howard left for the very last time in September, 1972. This time he never returned. Howard was in love with a younger and plainer woman, Judy Jenkinson. Ida referred to her as "the basketball player."

Ida and Rosalind Russell candid set photo

On the set *The Trouble With Angels* Rosalind, Ida
and William Frye Producer

Ida and crew on the set of *The Trouble With Angels*

"The Howie I knew and liked."

She would tell her friends, "Mr. Duff is now living with a basketball player!"

After all the great men she could have been with, and now this betrayal, Ida tried to stay busy with work. She made guest appearances on television shows and at industry events. Jack Warner and Ida made up for at least one evening as she attended "A Fifty-Year Salute to Warner Bros." Her recognizable voice was also heard in radio spots for the Crippled Children's Fund to help raise money. Ida appeared with actor Jimmy Stewart at the Golden Globe Awards as a presenter.

She socialized with Ralph Bellamy and Lorne Greene.

Ida flew to Kentucky to play the lead in *The Thoroughbreds*. She could not retain her lines, however, because she was preoccupied with her betrayal from Howard. Ida was then replaced by Vera Miles. Ida had never been released from a production before. She used to be a producer, so this was a great blow to her ego. Ida was very angry with the loss of this role, and would not allow Vera Miles' name to be mentioned in her presence.

"You do not fire Ida Lupino! The damn production can go to hell as far as I am concerned!"

In 1972 Ida gave yet another memorable performance in *Columbo*, with the late Johnny Cash, portraying his evangelist wife who is killed in a plane crash.

She also starred with Steve McQueen in *Junior Bonner*, as Elvira Bonner, the estranged wife of Ace Bonner, played by Robert Preston. She portrays Steve's mother. This movie was filmed in Arizona in 1972.

"I played Steve McQueen's mother, but I was only twelve years older than he was. Steve complained to Sam Peckinpah, our director, 'What's going on here? How can I look at Ida with those big blue eyes of hers and think of her as my mother?' I said. That's good because when I look at you, I am not thinking of you as a son."

"I loved the town of Prescott, Arizona. I had a wonderful time there with Steve. We went to the races. Steve and I won five races and came back with a small fortune. One of the horses was named Ida's Pet; it went on to become quite famous. When we returned, Sam was quite angry. He said, 'The next time you two go the races, take me!'

"Robert Preston would get loaded at night and try and come into my hotel room. I had to change rooms. The script called for me to slap him. I did, but I did not pull back the slap. I let Robert have it!

"Critics wrote that this was my come-back film. I never left; I was busy directing all of those years. It was my last important film role!"

"I made three other films but they were no damn good, *Food of the Gods*, where I am killed by a giant rat."

Ida, Ralph Bellamy and Lorne Greene

"Elvira and Ace Bonner"

"The rat was played by Howard Duff?" I asked Ida.

She broke up laughing, "A perfect role for him, darling. A big fat rat, type-casting! I had to keep doing that rat scene over and over, pretending the rat was there. It was difficult to keep doing!"

The *New York Times* dubbed *The Food of the Gods* "a stunningly ridiculous mixture of science fiction and horror film clichés."

"*The Devil's Rain*, where I play William Shatner's mother and I melt away—I replaced Mercedes McCambridge in this picture. Yes, that was me under all of that goo. I read a review about this film that it was so bad; the film critic said, 'Eddie Albert, Ida Lupino and Ernest Borgnine should buy up all of the prints and have them destroyed!'

"*My Boys are Good Boys*—I was so bored in this picture, I told the director to put me in the police car and drive me off of the set. He did!"

Ida Lupino's final guest-starring television appearance was in an episode of *Charlie's Angels*, in 1977. This incredible episode was written for Ida and appropriately titled, "I Will Be Remembered."

"I played an aging actress who is having financial troubles, much like myself at the time. Gloria Gibson, my character, is trying to make a return to films! She has a scheming agent. This was a well-written script. I have many great lines…"

GLORIA: "You don't know Hollywood…You don't climb your way to the top in this business, you claw your way. And, the ones you hurt…they never forget. They never forgive. No doubt they're quite pleased that I am broke and very close to losing this house."

GLORIA: "My dear, in the final analysis, directors are only another kind of audience; we are the creative artists. We shape and form them… watch me and you will know what acting is, on and off screen."

GLORIA: "Our inner selves are visible, and with them we overwhelm… We reduce you to your elements and then we rebuild you and return you to yourselves, our audience, remade, exalted and loyal to the stars they love and remember!"

Ida enjoyed reuniting with her old friends, such as Olivia de Havilland, during her retirement.

Mala Powers, Marie Windsor, Vincent Sherman, Roddy McDowall and Bea Arthur were all Ida's very close friends. They would often come for lunch and to parties at Ida's home.

Ida corresponded with long-time friend Barbara Stanwyck. They had the same hairdresser, Faye, who would come to their homes. Ida had directed episodes of *The Big Valley*, starring Barbara Stanwyck.

Barbara stated, "Ida could do it all!"

September 20, 1986

Dear Ida,

The long years I've been living abroad have been enriching
and rewarding, but there've been disadvantages, too, such
as losing touch with valued friends at home — and you are
one of these.

You were such good company when we worked together at Warner's, so imaginative and humorous, and had such a high ideal
of our profession and of personal relationships; I regret
not having been able to enjoy these qualities of yours since
then. What I also regret is that I missed seeing your fine
work as a director; how courageous and enterprising you were
to have undertaken this added career, and how well you suc-
ceeded in this difficult and challenging field.

When I'm next in Los Angeles, I'd love to see you — we have
an awful lot to catch up on!

Meanwhile, this brings you my warmest regards and good wishes,
together with much affection,

As always,

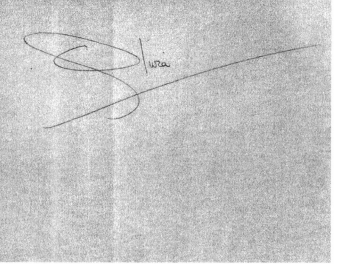

From Olivia to Ida 9/20/1986

156

Party for Ida – Celebrity Guests: Marie Windsor, Vincent Sherman, Mala Powers, Jack Hupp and Bea Arthur.
Photo Credit: Roddy McDowall

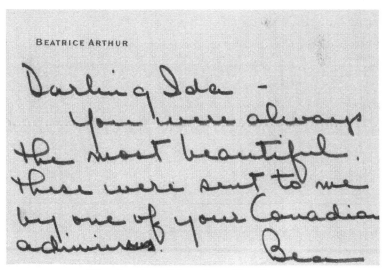

Handwritten Note from Bea Arthur

19

The Conservatorship of Ida Lupino

IDA VOLUNTEERED FOR A COURT-APPOINTED conservatorship in 1984, naming me as her conservator. My legal duties were to safeguard and protect Ida's assets, with Ida taking an acting interest in this process. She stated in court papers that she had not worked since 1977 and she was afraid her finances were dwindling, due to poor business dealings and her long separation from Howard Duff.

"My financial position was, to some degree, heavily controlled by a Business Manager, David Martin of Business Administration and to some extent a Lawyer, Mr. Robert Richland. Their bank did not keep in touch with me. I am no longer a child but an elderly woman in my sixties. I have earned my own way since I was thirteen years old. My health is to some degree 'shaky' as my work over many years has been heavy and much of it. Therefore medical help has been a must. I no longer have those I loved and completely trusted. They have all passed on. I have been a lost one, to be frank until I met you, Annie."

Ida's business manager, David Martin, had loaned Howard Duff $38,000.00 of Ida's money. Howard, though working on *Flamingo*

Road, was paying back this loan, interest free, and in monthly installments. Ida could have used this money to maintain her home.

Mala Powers (star of *Outrage*) stated to the press, "Ida's home was in a great need of repair. She was in trouble and needed help but Ida was too proud to ask her friends and family for assistance. Ida became friends with Mary Ann Anderson, whom she hired as her Secretary. Ida had complete faith and trust in Mary Ann."

Vincent Sherman (Director, *The Hard Way*): "I was happy to meet you Mary, and see Ida once again. There is still a special sweetness in Ida's face that I remember from the past. Above all, I have a good feeling about the two of you being together. When you help someone, as you are doing, it enlarges your own character and makes you a better person. We will all have lunch together again very soon. Give my love to Ida."

After a twelve year separation, Ida filed for divorce from Howard Duff. Ida's new attorney, Simon Taub, represented her. Ida's former attorney, Robert Richland, represented Howard. Ida gave up any or all claims she may have had to Howard's assets and to any future earnings of his; and Howard gave up any or all claims to any of Ida's assets or future earnings of hers. Ida wanted nothing from Howard and got nothing except for the Brentwood home located on Old Oak Lane that she bought and paid for when she was first married to him.

"Even the business marriage wasn't all that successful. We had our careers but I left mine for his! Howard's career was my own; it was my idea to make all of those sacrifices for him. He told me our marriage was a gross waste of time! That really hurt me. Well he wasn't worth it. I know it now!" Under the conservatorship, Ida retained her rights to make medical decisions, to vote, remarry, and to terminate the conservatorship order if she wished to (but she never did). Ida needed protection from the court and I wanted protection from Ida's estranged family. Howard Duff had the nerve to have me put under surveillance by a private investigator, even though I was bonded for one million dollars. Ida was furious when she heard about this! I met Duff once. He walked over to me and said, "Hi! I am Howard." I replied, "Hi! I am Mary Ann." He looked startled and walked away.

When any person is under a conservatorship, everything has to be approved by the court, and a yearly accounting filed. Old Oak Lane sold for $750,000.00. Ida received $500,000.00 down and carried a $250,000.00 First Trust deed when her Brentwood home sold. Now, she could live as a movie legend once more. Ida purchased, again, with court approval, 12220 Houston Street in North Hollywood for $250,000.00. It was a grand English Tudor house with hand-carved beamed ceilings and tastefully-ornate stained-glass windows. This house had everything but a swimming pool. With court approval once again, funds were approved for a new swimming pool to be built for $25,000.00.

Ida designed the shape of the pool and added brick trimming. She also wanted brick streamers in the cement decking around the pool. This was truly a movie star's home and pool.

The ex-Mrs. Duff left Brentwood, along with all of her wretched memories of Howard.

Ida embarked on a new life in the Valley, where I reunited her with Jim Barnet, a dear friend of hers from the early days of Warner Bros. Ida would invite Jim for holidays and parties.

One morning, I received a call from Jim. He was quite upset. "You better get over to Ida's immediately!"

"Why," I asked?

"A reporter from *The Sun* tabloid in Europe is heading over to Ida's. She stopped by here earlier looking for her. I will call Ida by phone to warn her, while you head over to Ida's house."

I left immediately for Ida's. Once I arrived in front of her gated home, I saw this short, stocky woman walking down the east side

of Ida's property. She was heading towards the back of Ida's house, decidedly trespassing! I got out of my car—ready for confrontation.

I called firmly out to her, "Stop," but she refused, continuing up the path. I ran up behind her and I grabbed the collar on the back of her imitation Colombo trench coat. I was much taller than this woman, so, looking down at her, I said pointedly, "You'd better not go in there! If you do, Miss Lupino will call the police and have you arrested!"

The reporter replied, "I am just here to do my job, to take a picture of the inside of Ida's house, and write a story about her for *The Sun*!"

Apparently, Jim had gotten hold of Ida by telephone because two of the upstairs dormer windows flew open and there was Ida Lupino, leaning intensively out of the second story window!

This reporter, apprehensively uttered, "Is that Ida Lupino?"

"Yes it is!" said Ida in a booming, authoritative voice. "Hit her on the point, Annie! Hit her on the point right here!"

Ida pointed with her right finger to her right chin. "Hit her right here!"

The woman started to tremble so I let go of the collar on her Colombo coat and she took off running.

Ida later told me hitting someone 'on the point' was a stage direction that she gave to actors in fight scenes when she directed westerns.

The retired Ida still remained a masterful director.

On one occasion Ida's cat, Timothy, got stuck in a tree in her back yard and could not come down. Ida gave me directions on how to climb the tree. She would tell me which branches to put my feet on and how to climb down with her precious kitty.

With Ida finally divorcing Howard and requesting a conservator at the same time, she was once again sought after by the tabloids—this time, by *The National Enquirer*. It was at this point, Ida decided to write her memoirs. "These tabloids never get anything right," quipped Ida.

"They never get my birth year correct, 1918, or my age correct. I am not eighty-seven years old! They can't even write! They have me cleaning garbage eighteen hours per day. I have a question for you, Annie." Ida starts to break up laughing, "How does anyone clean garbage?"

I start to laugh and reply, "They don't!"

"They also have me sitting on top of my roof in my director's chair, firing on my neighbors. Annie darling, can you imagine me up on my roof firing at my neighbors? The roof is slanted. I would fall off!"

"Well Ida, yes I could!" Ida smiles.

"I wouldn't even use them for toilet paper, it would infect me!"

Ida dancing the tango with a young entertainer.

Ida would look through her collection of old, rare, candid photo stills and magazines. She would make comments. I would ask her questions about her life and career and record her on tape.

The first question I asked Ida was, "If you had to do it over again would you have been an actress?"

"Annie, I never had a childhood. I didn't play with dolls. I was busy playing hookers! I know what it is like to do something you do not want to do. I was forced into being an actress and I didn't want to be. If I had to do it all over again, I'd do it differently. I would sit home, write lyrics, and own a bake shop!"

Ida was a grand storyteller, often revealing quite incredible ideas and scenarios. She was extremely witty with her underlining sarcasm. Ida had a fascination with current religious implications of various sensational events of the day. She had a series of political convictions and she would share these with you at length. These were well grounded in current events and passionately held, determinedly given.

Ida had a very strong opinion of television shows that were being aired at the time. Her favorite shows: *Hawaii Five-0*, *Mission Impossible*, *Barney Miller*, *Murder, She Wrote* and *The Golden Girls*. Ida did not care much for *Mork and Mindy*. "They're out!" When she was reviewing her *TV Guide* and would come across a film starring Ida Lupino, she would state, "This probably isn't very good, this film with Ida Lupino," when, indeed, it was!

In person, she was knowingly madcap and utterly charming. Ida was the original Auntie Mame.

Ida with Barbara Stanywck.

21
The End Is Known

IN NOVEMBER 1993, NEW YORK AFTRA presented Ida with its second annual WIN (Woman's Image Now) Award because "she is a major force and an inspiration to all women by breaking barriers, setting precedents and being responsible for achievements by women in the entertainment arts." Those are the words of Elaine Le Garo, Chair of New York AFTRA's Women Committee.

Ida had planned to attend this event. First-class airplane tickets had been purchased on American Airlines and hotel reservations had been made. However, due to severe weather conditions, Ida asked Mala Powers, who starred in her production of *Outrage*, to accept the honors for her. Mala had an apartment in New York and was there at the time of this award benefit. Ann Sperber, author of the Edward R. Murrow book and a New York resident would attend the event. Ann had recently interviewed Ida for her up-and-coming book on Humphrey Bogart.

Robert Osborne, gossip column writer for *The Hollywood Reporter*, wrote in his Wednesday, November 17, 1993, column about

The End is Known

the event. He stated, "knowing Lupino, she'd doubtless still be in there pitching if ill health had not zapped her energies." Ida took great offense to this and sent Robert Osborne a telegram stating, "I am not in fragile health nor has my health zapped my energy, get your facts straight or are you ill?"

Osborne responded after a complaint was made to the editor of *The Hollywood Reporter* on Ida's behalf. Osborne stated that, "Inadvertently I hit a nerve when I wrote about the great accomplishments of Ida Lupino and her myriad of supreme accomplishments as an actress-director-producer. Lupino sent me a blistering mailgram to let me know that she took offense to a mention about her fragile health."

"He mentioned in this retraction that I was indignant."

Previously, in 1987, Olivia de Havilland had been in town to present the award for Artistry in Cinematography and was escorted to the 75th Academy Award ceremony by Robert Osborne. They did not skip the awards to visit Ida in the hospital, as stated by Robert Osborne in an interview for a book titled *Women of Warner Brothers* and written by Daniel Bubbeo for McFarland Publishing in 2000.

Olivia came to visit Ida prior. I would pick up Olivia at The Beverly Hills Hotel and drive her to Saint Johns Hospital, in Santa Monica. Ida had been hospitalized after suffering a stroke. Thankfully, this stroke left Ida's speech unimpaired, so she was still able to communicate with ease.

These two great actresses performed scenes from *Devotion*, where they portrayed sisters Charlotte and Emily Bronte. The Catholic Nuns at Saint John's Hospital were so captivated by Olivia's and Ida's grand performances that they actually believed they really were sisters!

Emily and Charlotte Bronte

The truth be told, Ida was hospitalized for forty-one days, not several months as reported by Osborne. Ida had a large private suite at Saint John's Hospital, across the hall from where Bette Davis had recently stayed.

The head nurse on the floor told me if Bette Davis checked back in to the hospital she was going to put Bette in with Ida. I told this nurse you may not have any hospital left!

Ida was recuperating from the side effects of a stroke. She had been a heavy smoker throughout her life. Robert Osborne never visited Ida, as he stated. If Osborne had appeared at the hospital to see Ida, she would have thrown him out of her room personally!

"He never liked me. He called me 'the hard luck' Lupino on his show for Turner Classic Movies!"

After Ida's lengthy stay at Saint John's Hospital, she needed some intensive physical therapy; so, instead of staying any longer in the hospital, Ida wanted to leave because Ava Gardner had checked in. A nurse had asked Ida if she wanted to see Ava Gardner.

"No, I do not!"

"Why not?" asked the nurse.

"She is an Earthquake!"

Ida went out to the Motion Picture Country Home. Her private monthly cost there was $8,000.00.

Actress Mae Clarke, better known for getting a 'grapefruit in the face' by James Cagney in the film *The Public Enemy*, was the reigning Queen at the Motion Picture Country Home.

Well, that all changed when Ida Lupino arrived. I would go every day to see her. One evening while I was there visiting Ida, Mae showed up outside Ida's suite and accused Ida of stealing her false teeth.

Ida replied, "Mae why in the hell would I want your damn false teeth, when I have my own teeth?"

Mae insisted, "Ida you stole them, I know you did. You do not want me to be able to talk!'

"That is ridiculous, but you do sound funny!" Ida replied.

These two verbally battled back and forth, which led to a grand shoving match. Finally, Ida got bored. She wanted to 'wrap up' this scene. Ida yelled to me, "Annie, get me a grapefruit!"

We all broke up laughing, including Mae and a very large nurse who had been searching the grounds looking for Mae. This nurse escorted Mae Clarke back to her room in The Loge section of the Motion Picture Country Home.

Ida continued to entertain everyone at the Motion Picture Country Home. One afternoon, the telephone kept ringing and ringing in the Chaplin's office, so Ida graciously went in and answered it, "Whore House!"

Ida's physical therapy regiment was up, and it was time for her to leave. Before she did, she donated many of her old awards to the Motion Picture Country Home. Her awards and photos were placed on a large wall across from their intensive care unit. Ida came to the unveiling before she left and proclaimed to all, "I am so intensive! Good Bye."

Ida returned to her home in the Valley, but her awards still remain on display there today!

Within a few months, Olivia returned to Los Angeles. She arranged a dinner at the very chic and expensive French restaurant La Sere, in Sherman Oaks, for Ida, in celebration of her recovery. I was a guest; Robert Osborne was not.

Claims that "The final blow for Ida was when Howard Duff died of a massive heart attack on July 9, 1990" were absolutely false! Ida was the one who filed for divorce. She had been involved with Jim Barnett since 1984. "I used to answer her telephone in her dressing room at Warner Bros. Studios. Her telephone was always ringing!"

Jim had created the television series *F Troop*, and he later wrote the movie of the week, *Death At Love House*, which starred Robert Wagner and Kate Jackson. Jim was retired but continued to perform legal arbitration for The Writer's Guild.

Vincent Sherman said, "Before the Telluride Festival, I received a phone call from Mary. She had been keeping me informed about Ida's health and activities during the past and now regretted to tell me that Ida had recently been diagnosed with colon cancer. Ida had asked to see me. We all met for lunch. Ida looked better than I had seen her in a long time. We spent a delightful afternoon together, laughing and joking about the past. Mary told me later it was one of the best afternoons she had ever had. I was happy to hear that."

Ida resting with her Burmese kitty named "Collie"

Ida, jokingly, told Vincent she got the 'Big C' from all of the bad scripts she had to digest at Warner Bros.

Vincent replied, "That is a possibility!"

With many doctor appointments and tests performed at Saint Joseph Hospital, located in Burbank, I hired a driver and limousine for Ida. I would accompany her. After her appointments and tests were completed, we would have lunch at Chadney's, across from NBC Studios. On the way home, Ida's driver, Dale, would drive us through Griffith Park and out to The Los Angeles Equestrian Center. Ida loved to see the horses and watch the jumping events.

In 1995, while Ida was bravely fighting colon cancer and needing all of her energy to do so, a 'so called' admirer of hers, William Donati, wrote an unauthorized book about her. His book was titled *Charming Mad Woman* and was to be published by The University of Kentucky Press. With court approval, Ida retained additional legal counsel, spending $10,000 to have Mr. Donati's false writings removed from his book, including changing the title.

Ida prevailed. "Donati is a smiler with a knife!" Donati had once been a guest in her home for Christmas. Ida felt betrayed.

Director Louis Antonelli, based in the windy city of Chicago, contacted Ida through me and The Director's Guild. Mr. Antonelli wanted Ida's permission to restore her classic film noir *The Hitch-Hiker*. Ida's response to me at first was, "Why in the hell would Mr. Antonelli want to waste his time restoring that damn old film of mine? Why doesn't he restore something else? I had nothing but trouble making that picture! Everyone was against it"... Ida begins to laugh... "but we made it any way!"

Louis Antonelli said, "In December 1992 as Ida's 75th birthday was approaching, I got the idea to reintroduce The Hitch-Hiker to Ida with a new twist; what if we embark on a full restoration of *The Hitch-Hiker*? Make it shine, Ida and be exactly like you always wanted it to be with no compromises? Upon speaking to her about it I was met with the true Lupino fury."

"Why do you care about that old junk, when no one cares about it? Leave it alone!'

"This was her sharp reply! I tried to reason with her, that in truth many people cared. Ida would have none of it."

"As the weeks progressed into early 1993, Ida changed about the project, in the nature of her generous heart, her concern was that I should in any way not waste my own valuable time on anything to do with one of her 'forgotten films,' when I had fresh pictures of my own to create and exhibit. I assured Ida that my work to bring back *The Hitch-Hiker* would not impede my own films in any way and it would be a real honor to do this project but only with her blessing."

"Ida was deeply touched by this and reluctantly agreed to let me try. Always budget conscious, Ida made me assure her that I would not spend my 'good money' for this 'foolish' but 'very dear effort of yours.'"

Ida and Louis bonded over the phone, one director to another. He had such deep admiration and respect for her. Ida finally approved *The Hitch-Hiker* restoration. She was very touched by Louis' knowledge of this film and of her entire career. Lou's project restored not only *The Hitch-Hiker*, but Ida's faith in others, for film projects, as well. After her horrible betrayal from Donati and his dreadful book, this was a project that Ida could be proud of! Sadly, she never got to view the final restored print.

Angela Lansbury also contacted Ida about an appearance on her show, *Murder She Wrote*. Ida wanted to do a segment with Angela. She hoped to play a bag lady who finds a dead body on the beach and helps solve the murder.

Warren Beatty contacted me about a project for Ida. He had produced a movie of the week starring Katherine Hepburn and wanted to use Ida in a new project. Unfortunately, Ida could not be a part of this, either.

Ida suffered a mild stroke after a surprise visit from her daughter, Bridget. They had not seen each other for over a decade. She continued to visit her mother on a daily basis. Bridget would sit quietly in the corner of Ida's bedroom and observe. Ida's sister Rita would visit as well.

Ida knew her time was limited, and her concern was growing stronger about death and dying. She became very anxious.

"To put a great many obstacles to one side and feel more at peace about having to go from this life is a persistent thought in the wakening hours and there have been many. I hope to leave this life peacefully and in my own home and my bed, not some damn hospital, where they wake you up at night to give you a sleeping pill. Annie will see to this, I know!"

I telephoned the Reverend Doctor Robert H. Schuller. Ida would watch him faithfully on television. He returned my call personally. I explained to him Ida's situation. He was a great fan of hers and asked to see Ida.

"Yes, please come," I told him.

Reverend Schuller spent an afternoon visiting with Ida. He helped comfort her anxieties about death and made her laugh.

"Ida if I was younger I would make a picture with you!"

She loved hearing that! Ida instructed me to make a large donation to The Crystal Cathedral for her as Dr. Schuller was leaving. I did!

During her final days, Ida reminisced about her father, Stanley, who was one of Britain's most celebrated comedians. "Stanley, who could also write a play and fit it with workman-like lyrics," Ida said. "My father had a great comeback line in his musical comedy *Over She Goes* (1930), when champion-boxer-turned-actor Max Baer challenges Stanley to a fight. He makes him a generous offer of letting him have the first two punches. My father Stanley's great reply, 'I am not worried about the first two punches. It is the fourth!'"

Ida's father wrote his autobiography, entitled *From The Stocks To The Stars*. The following is a summary from his original manuscript:

Stanley was born in London, May 15, 1884. Stanley, the cousin of Lupino Lane, belonged to the stage from the time his mother, Florence Webster, took him, as a child of four, to his father's dressing room at the Royale Theatre on Drury Lane. After some training from his father, George Lupino, Stanley had his debut at age six. Three years later, after the death of his mother, he joined a traveling troupe, which played in the English provenances.

After eight weeks of employment, the troupe found itself stranded in York. Penniless, Stanley had to walk back to London, earning his way singing and entertaining. In London, he obtained work at the Wonderland, where for five shillings a week he boxed four rounds nightly.

The young Stanley retired from the ring after several bad beatings and the loss of six teeth. Returning to the stage, Stanley substituted for his brother, Barry Lupino, in *Sleeping Beauty*.

The next eight years (1915-1923) Stanley starred in a number of shows. Stanley passed away in London, on June 10, 1942, at age fortyeight, from cancer. He is buried in the Lambeth Cemetery on Blackshaw Road in England.

Ida spoke about her precious little mother, Connie, who was killed in a tragic three-car collision near Baker on Highway 91. "It was Christmas Day, I was expecting my mum to join me for the holidays. I felt a chill, an icy feeling, the telephone rang. My mum had been in an accident. I left immediately to go to her!"

Connie Gladys Lupino died on December 26, 1959, at the Barstow Community Hospital. Ida was at her bedside when she died. "The doctors thought she was getting better." Ida never fully recovered from the loss of her mother; she was her best friend. Connie's funeral service was at Wee Kirk o' the Heather at Forest Lawn in Glendale. Connie, not Ida, is buried next to Errol Flynn. Collier Young and Joan Fontaine attended Connie's service: "I was very fond of Connie!" - Joan Fontaine

Ida Lupino passed away at her home in Burbank Rancho, California, on August 3, 1995, from a major stroke, while battling colon cancer.

One of the very last things Ida said, while looking at a picture of her father was, "Stanley, I hope I made you proud!"

Ida was the greatest Lupino of them all! Stanley would be very proud.

A Celebration of Life was given in Ida's honor at the home of Mala Powers. Ida had stated earlier, "If you give me a funeral I will not go!" Barbara Hale, Vincent Sherman, Marie Windsor, Roddy McDowall, Louis Antonelli, along with Ida's sister Rita and Ida's daughter Bridget all spoke. Bea Arthur was filled with emotion and walked out. Lovely white flowers filled the rooms. The delicate white roses sent from Olivia de Havilland were placed next to Ida's urn. An after party was 'privately' held on Mala's patio for Ida's closest friends, her "chums."

Vincent Sherman said, "It was a fitting tribute to one of the great talents of our time."

Ida Lupino was seventy-seven years old when she left us and will be remembered always, in her many brilliant screen performances as the tough girl moll with a heart of gold and in her incredible directorial work breaking all barriers as a woman director with a vision.

"Where there is human courage, there is drama. When every day people fight for life and love, you have the very essence of heroism. I tried to capture this in every film I directed."

Afterword

"I WAS NOW ABLE TO TELL WARNER BROS. to go to hell! None of us were happy there. I used to go up on the hill behind the studio and throw rocks at it. I was always going on suspension or doing roles that I absolutely hated. I would refuse to do roles turned down by other actresses."

Competition by another actress, I asked? "No!"

"And I never said I was the poor man's Bette Davis. Warner Bros. came up with that bad line, not me. I respected Davis. I did say jokingly that Bette Davis could do the housework!" - Ida Lupino

"She couldn't work anywhere during suspension, so she would go on sets of movies. Most of the directors knew her and liked her and she would watch them direct." - Mala Powers

"They gave Bette Davis first choice of all of the parts. Then they would hand something over to Ida, something she did not want to play.

Collier and Ida wed in 1948

Vincent Sherman said, "Ida could have done anything Davis could do, heavy, light… She had a great sense of scene construction. If only Ida could have gotten another picture like *They Drive By Night* or *The Hard Way*, she could have stayed on top!"

Ida adds, "Acting is a born talent within people, it can be polished and made better but you definitely cannot teach someone to act; to be real, to be that person. I left it up to the audience, if I reached them playing that character. Actor's acting, Orson Welles, I am bored. Katherine Hepburn, an original, no one could copy her!"

After *Not Wanted* and *Outrage*, Ida had offers by all the studios as a director, but she remained independent. Although Collier and Ida were divorced in 1951, they continued to work together for three more years.

"To this day Collier is still the man I love. He was my favorite husband. It was a divorce that neither one of us wanted! Collie and I kept working together because we were in such rapport about the movies we wanted to make. We were always looking for true life material. We based our premises on people we talked to or things that really happened! Collie died in a car crash on Christmas Day in 1980."

When Filmakers dissolved, Ida turned her full attention to television directing. I asked Ida if she remembered her first directorial assignment? "Do I remember my first assignment? Do I! It was *Have Gun Will Travel*. Richard Boone (Paladin) was a wonderful man, but he was not out to baby any director, believe me; but after the first episode he said, 'I like you, I want you on the rest of them.' I stayed on and directed four episodes."

Richard Boone, who liked his direction hard-boiled, wanted Ida for her first *Have Gun Will Travel* directorial assignment to shoot a script written by Harry Fink, famed for his graphic descriptions of physical violence, which included rape, murder and sandstorms.

Ida held the record for directing the most episodes of television through the 1980s. As a director, Ida worked on fifty-six different television series. She brought shows in under budget, and was highly respected by veteran crews. She was referred to as the female "Hitch." Ida handled all kind of material in the 1960s—suspense, thriller, mystery, comedy, and action.

"Directing keeps you in a constant state of first-night nerves. You may be terrified at first but you must not let it show on the set. Nothing

On the set of *Have Gun Will Travel*

goes according to Hoyle. Reshuffle your schedule. Keep your sense of humor. Don't panic. I sometimes wonder how anything gets on film!"

Ida Lupino's television work expanded her range of directorial work from a social realist to westerns, tales of the supernatural, situation comedies, murder mysteries and gangster stories. This revealed a proud woman director, ambitious with her camera and technically way ahead of her time.

"I loved shooting for television. I'd learned to shoot lean and fast in the 1950s. In television there's no running over. If you are slow and go over budget, you will get fired. I loved the tension and the excitement and the people. Each show was a new challenge to Mother!"

"Cut and print!"

Filmography

... as a Film Actress

Love Race (1931) Lupino Lane (cameo)

Her First Affair (1932) St. George's Production (Sterling Film Co.)

Money For Speed (1933) Hallmark Films (United Artist)

High Finance (1933) First National-British)

The Ghost Camera (1933) Julius Hagen-Twickenham Production)

I Lived With You (1933) Twickenham films (Gaumont-British)

Prince of Arcadia (1933) Nettlefold-Fogwell Production (Gaumont-British)

Search for Beauty (1934) Paramount

Come On Marines (1934) Paramount

Ready for Love (1934) Paramount

Paris In Spring (1935) Paramount

Smart Girl (1935) Paramount

Peter Ibbetson (1935) Paramount

Anything Goes (1936) Paramount

One Rainy Afternoon (1936) Pickford-Lasky (United Artists)

Yours for The Asking (1936) Paramount

The Gay Desperado (1936) Pickford-Lasky (United Artist)

Sea Devils (1937) RKO

Let's Get Married (1937) Columbia

Artists and Models (1937) Paramount

Fight for your Lady (1937) RKO

The Lone Spy Hunt (1939) Columbia

The Lady and the Mob (1939) Columbia

The Adventures of Sherlock Holmes (1939) Twentieth Century Fox

The Light That Failed (1939) Paramount

They Drive By Night (1940) Warner Bros. – First National

High Sierra (1941) Warner Bros. First National

Out of the Fog (1941) Warner Bros. – First National

Ladies in Retirement (1941) Columbia

Moontide (1942) Twentieth Century Fox

The Hard Way (1942) Warner Bros. – First National Pictures

Life Begins At 8:30 (1942) Twentieth Century Fox

Forever and A Day (1943) RKO

Thank you Lucky Stars (1943) Warner Bros. Warner Bros. First National

Hollywood Canteen (1944) Warner Bros. – First National

In Our Time (1944) Warner Bros. – First National

Pillow to Post (1945) Warner Bros. – First National Devotion (1946)
    Warner Bros. – First National

The Man I Love (1946) Warner Bros. – First National

*Escape Me Never (*1947) Warner Bros. – First National

Deep Valley (1947) Warner Bros. – First National

Road House (1948) Twentieth Century Fox

Lust for Gold (1949) Columbia

Woman In Hiding (1949) Universal

The Hard Way

On Dangerous Ground (1951) RKO

Beware My Lovely (1952) FilmakersRKO

Jennifer (1953) Allied Artists

The Bigamist (1953) Filmakers

Private Hell 36 (1954) Filmakers

Woman's Prison (1955) Bryan Foy Production – Columbia

The Big Knife (1955) Associates and Aldrich Co. –United Artist

While The City Sleeps (1956) RKO

Strange Intruder (1956) A Lindsly Parsons Production – Allied Artists

Backtrack (1969) MCA-TV Universal

Deadhead Miles (1972) Biplane Cinematograph Production– Paramount

Woman In Chains (1972) Paramount TV for ABC

190

Junior Bonner (1972) ABC Pictures Corp. – Joe Wizan-Booth Gardner,
    Production – Solar Production Cinerama
Strangers In 7A (1972) Carliner Productions for CBS-TV
Female Artillery (1973) Universal TV for ABC-TV
I Love A Mystery (1973) NBC-TV
The Letters (1973) Spelling-Goldberg Productions for ABC-TV
The Devil's Rain (1975) Sandy Howard Production –Bryanston
Food of the Gods (1976) American International
My Boys Are Good Boys (1978) Lone Star Pictures

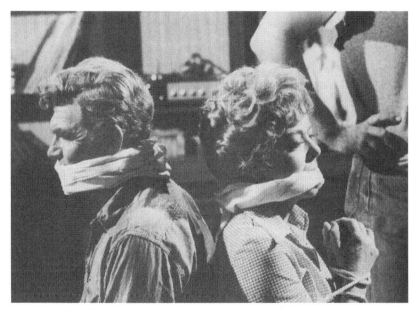

The Strangers in 7A

...as a Television Actress

Four Star Playhouse 12/31/53 to 7/1956
Ford Theatre 2/25/54 5/6/54
Mr. Adams and Eve 1957 to 1958 (episodes)
Lux Playhouse 2/20/59

The Lucy/Desi Comedy Hour 6/6/59 ("Lucy's Summer Vacation")

The Twilight Zone 10/23/59

Note: Ida Lupino was the only woman to star in and direct an episode.

Bonanza 10/24/59

G.E. Theatre 2/26/61

Frontier Justice 8/31/61

The Investigators 12/21/61

Sam Benedict 1/5/62

Death Valley Days 1962

The Virginian 3/20/63

Kraft Suspense Theatre 11/14/63

Burke's Law 11/4/64

The Rogues 11/8/64

The Virginian 4/21/64

The Wild, Wild West 10/7/66

Judd for the Defense 2/9/68

Batman 3/7/68

It Takes A Thief 4/2/68

The Outcasts 2/17/69

Mod Squad 3/18/69

The Name of the Game 11/13/70

Nanny and the Professor 2/12/71

Columbo 1/19/72

Alias Smith and Jones 2/24/72

Medical Center 3/1/72

The Strangers in 7A 10/14/72

The Bold Ones 12/26/72

Female Artillery 1/2/26/72

I Love A Mystery 1/2/73

The Letters 3/6/73

Barnaby Jones 8/31/74

The Streets of San Francisco 1/24/74
Columbo 3/3/74
Manhunter 3/11/74
Ellery Queen 9/18/75
Switch 9/30/75
Police Woman 10/10/75
Charlie's Angels 3/9/77

... with Filmakers

Not Wanted (1949) Emerald Productions Film Classics
Never Fear (1949) Filmakers Eagle Lion Films
Outrage (1950) Filmakers RKO
Hard Fast and Beautiful (1951) Filmakers – RKO
Beware My Lovely (1952) Filmakers RKO
The Hitch-Hiker (1953) Filmakers RKO
The Bigamist (1953) Filmakers RKO
Private Hell 36 (1954) Filmakers RKO

The stars Clarke, Ryan, Greer, Forrest and Lupino of *Hard Fast and Beautiful* Back Stage San Francisco World Wide Tour

Major Film Directorial Credits:

The Trouble with Angels (1965) Columbia Pictures

Television Directorial Credits:

Screen Director's Playhouse 1/18/56

On Trial 11/23/56

The Donna Reed Show 12/10/56

Tate 9/21/60

Have Gun Will Travel 4/3/59 4/9/60 6/1/60

Hotel de Paree 2/5/60

The Untouchables 12/4/62 3/5/63 5/7/63

Thriller 1961-1962

The Fugitive 11/19/63 12/3/63 1/14/64

Bewitched 1/10/65

The Rogues 12/10/63   2/7/65

The Twilight Zone 3/20/64 (Note: Ida Lupino was the only woman to
     direct an episode.)

Dundee and the Culhane 10/4/67

The Virginian 11/9/66

Bob Hope Presents The Chrysler Theatre 5/11/66

Daniel Boone 10/19/67

The Ghost and Mrs. Muir 1968

Alfred Hitchcock Presents 12/6/60 1/24/61

Mr. Novak 3/24/64 3/2/65 12/3/65

Breaking Point 2/13/63

Dr. Kildare 2/13/63

Kraft Suspense Theatre 3/12/64

Gilligan's Island 10/17/64 10/24/64 10/3/66

Ida directing *The Donna Reed Show*

Ida and Chuck Connors

The following are television episodes directed by Ida Lupino as a guest director, but the Director's Guild did not have official records:

G.E. Theatre
Hong Kong
The Road West
The Big Valley
Gunsmoke
Nanny and the Professor
Sam Benedict
77 Sunset Strip
The Bill Cosby Show
Honey West
Temple Houston
The Rifleman

On the set—Ida and Roger Smith,
77 Sunset Strip

Radio Appearances

1944	*Screen Guild Players* "High Sierra"
1944	*Suspense* "The Sisters"
1953	*Stars Over Hollywood* "Chasten Thy Son"

Awards and Tributes

Lupino has two stars on the Hollywood Walk of Fame for television and film located at 1724 Vine Steet and 6821 Hollywood Blvd.

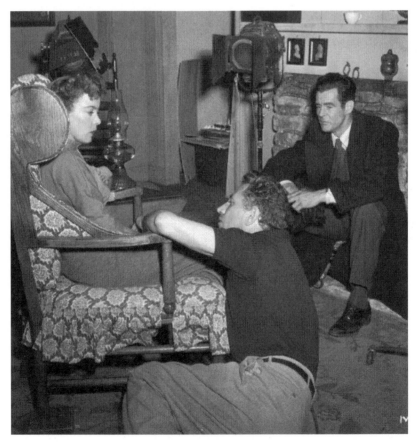

Ida being directed by Nichlos Reye *On Dangerous Ground*
with Robert Ryan

Index